The Pony Club
Stoneleigh Park
Kenilworth
Warwickshire
CV8 2RW

Website: www.pcuk.org

The Pony Club Guide to Bits & Bitting
is published by The Pony Club

British Library Cataloguing in Publication Data.
A catalogue record for this book is available from the British Library.

ISBN 978-1-907279-18-8

Director of Publications: Nikki Herbert BHSI

Design and Production: Paul G. Harding
www.hardingbooks.com

Printed by Halstan Printing Group in Amersham, UK
www.halstan.co.uk

Trade distribution by Kenilworth Press
An imprint of Quiller Publishing Ltd.
Wykey House, Wykey, Shrewsbury, SY4 1JA
Tel: 01939 261616 Fax: 01939 261606
Email: info@quillerbooks.com
Website: www.kenilworthpress.co.uk

The Pony Club Guide to

Bits & Bitting

by Carolyn Henderson
with photographs by John Henderson

Contents

1. A Bit of Communication

A horse jumping happily in a pelham.

Riding is all about communication with your horse, whether you're enjoying your first lessons or competing in the Pony Club Championships. Choosing the right bit and using it correctly plays a vital part.

When you look at how many types of bit are available, it can seem to be a complicated subject—but although there are lots of factors to take into account, it doesn't have to be confusing. Bitting is a skill, but it's one that anyone can learn and the ground rules are always the same:

- The rider must be in control and able to communicate with the horse in the kindest and most efficient way.
- Your horse must be comfortable and happy. Bitting isn't the only factor that will influence this, but it can play an important part. You'll also find that if your horse is comfortable and happy, control and communication will be easier to achieve!
- The bit must be suitable for the shape of the horse's mouth, the level of his training and the rider's ability.
- It must be the correct size and be correctly adjusted.
- As with all tack and equipment, it may need to comply with rules and competition regulations. This applies not just to the Pony Club, but to other organisations.
- You need to understand whether its action will be affected by other tack, such as a design of noseband or a martingale, so that you can look at the overall picture. Again, Pony Club and competition rules may apply.

- You may need to use different bits for different situations. For instance, most riders will be able to find a snaffle that meets competition requirements for dressage and will be able to use it for schooling on the flat. But there's nothing wrong with using a different bit for jumping or for hacking out if your horse becomes more forward going and it enables you to stay in control without having to use unacceptably strong rein aids.

Taking Up the Reins

It's important to understand how you use a bit to communicate with your horse. In simple terms, when we apply rein aids, we apply pressure on the bit. This should always be light—think in terms of applying a light touch—and should never cause the horse discomfort.

The starting point is an elastic contact, which tells the horse: 'I'm here, please listen to me.' You can only achieve this when the horse is going forward in an active way, but without tension; it does not come from taking a backwards feel on the rein. It's rather like holding hands with someone in a soft, consistent hold, without one person grabbing at the other's hand or occasionally dropping the hold without realising.

Pressure on its own won't work—it will just confuse the horse. Pressure and release, whether within your elastic contact or in the context of giving and picking up a loose rein, will. The pressure is your instruction to the horse and the release is the signal that he has done as you asked.

The pressure should be as light as possible and only be applied for a short period. A good rider on a well-schooled horse can communicate via the rein and other aids in a split second, so the aids may seem invisible. If a horse is not so well schooled, your aids may need to be more obvious, but they should never be harsh and you should always aim to refine them.

Don't assume that a new bit could be the answer to any problem, or that it could work miracles. Bitting is just one piece, though an important one, in the riding and horse care jigsaw. There is no such thing as a magic bit, though it may be that trying a different bit will make communication easier at a particular stage of your partnership.

If your horse is resisting your rein aids, which can cover everything from setting his jaw and/or opening his mouth to becoming strong when jumping, then of course you need to make sure that you are in control.

There are many reasons why a horse may resist the bit.

A change of bit may help, but mouth resistances can be a horse's way of expressing that he's uncomfortable or unable to do as his rider asks.

It might be simply that he finds it difficult at that stage of his schooling and that as he progresses, he will find it easier. Alternatively, he might be showing that you are asking him in a way that makes him uncomfortable, or that he has discomfort in his mouth.

It may also be that he is experiencing discomfort or pain in another part of his body that is totally unrelated to the bit. Demonstrating resistance, whether this be through evading the bit, napping, bucking or other forms of behaviour, is the only way he can show you that things are not right.

We all want to be kind to our horses and bits are often classified as being mild or severe. It may be a cliché to say that a bit is only as mild or severe as the hands on the reins, but it's also true. It's better to use a potentially stronger bit in a gentle way than to use a 'mild' one roughly.

You may be tempted to try a particular type of bit because a top rider or a friend thinks that it has helped solve a problem or improved a horse's way of going. Again, look at the overall picture.

This is where a knowledgeable eye on the ground is invaluable. In particular, a good instructor will help solve rider and schooling problems and a vet with a special interest in equine dentistry or a British Equine Veterinary Association-approved equine dental technician will check for and treat dental problems.

Rider preference may also come into play. We all aim to have an elastic contact with the horse's mouth, but some experienced riders find that certain types of bit suit their riding style. Some prefer bits that remain relatively still in the horse's mouth, whilst others always start by using a bit with more play.

It isn't that one design is necessarily better than another, just that it complements the way they school and produce their horses or their perception of what seems right. If a good rider knows that using an eggbutt snaffle, which stays still in the horse's mouth, always tempts him or her to fiddle with the reins, it may be better to use a loose ring version, which is more mobile.

A loose ring snaffle (top) is more mobile than an eggbutt snaffle (bottom).

A Good Mouth

Riders often talk about a horse having a good (or soft) mouth or a bad (or hard) mouth. Strictly speaking, neither are accurate descriptions, but are general terms used to describe a horse's way of going. It is usually understood that a horse with a good mouth is relaxed in his jaw and responsive to the rein aids and that one with a bad mouth is resistant and/or unresponsive.

Whilst horses have different physical characteristics, as explained later in this chapter, they all have the potential to be responsive and submissive to the rider's aids. Submission is a term used in dressage tests at all levels and doesn't mean that a horse is being forced or bullied. It means that he is obedient, but also willing, accepting and confident.

A good mouth isn't something a horse either has or lacks naturally, it's something that he acquires through education and being ridden correctly. The right bit can definitely help you achieve that responsiveness, but it will only help if it is used in the right way. A young horse has to be taught first of all to accept a bit in his mouth, then to stop, start and steer in answer to the rider's aids, of which the rein aids are just a small part.

The farther his education progresses, the more subtle those aids will become. Unfortunately, it's too easy to become fixated on our hands rather than what we're doing with the rest of our bodies!

Don't assume that because a horse is unresponsive, he has a bad or 'hard' mouth. He may not understand what you are asking him to do, or he may have been ridden in a way that has dulled his responsiveness, perhaps by someone who uses the reins to try and stay secure in the saddle or who gives conflicting signals without realising. If you're not sure, get advice from a good trainer. It's possible to re-educate a horse who has been ridden badly, though it can take a lot of time, patience and skill.

It's also important to differentiate between a horse who is strong and/or excited and one who is unbalanced and on the forehand. If you can't tell the difference, chances are that you may not be able to adjust your riding or, perhaps, choose a bit that will improve the situation.

A horse who feels heavy in your hand because he is leaning on the bit needs schooling so that he is able to engage his hindquarters and hindlegs and lift his abdominal muscles. This will enable him to push himself along from behind. In turn, this will see his forehand lighten and you will have an elastic but not heavy feel in the rein.

A particular bit—for example, a loose ring snaffle of some kind—may help to discourage him from leaning, as explained in Chapter 4, but only correct schooling and riding can improve his way of going.

A horse who is excited may want to go faster than you do or may show other resistances such as snatching at the reins and generally moving in directions other than the one you're aiming for! Whilst you must have control and a different bit and/or noseband may help, you need to work on getting the horse to listen to you. A good instructor will be able to help by looking at everything from your horse's lifestyle to exercises and techniques to focus his attention and help him become more submissive.

Last but never least, check that you are not inadvertently causing a problem or making it worse. Common scenarios are the rider who fiddles with the reins to try and get the horse to work in an outline, or one who takes a strong, constant hold against an onward bound horse. As always, ask a good instructor for help.

Correct schooling will help you keep an onward bound horse obedient and balanced.

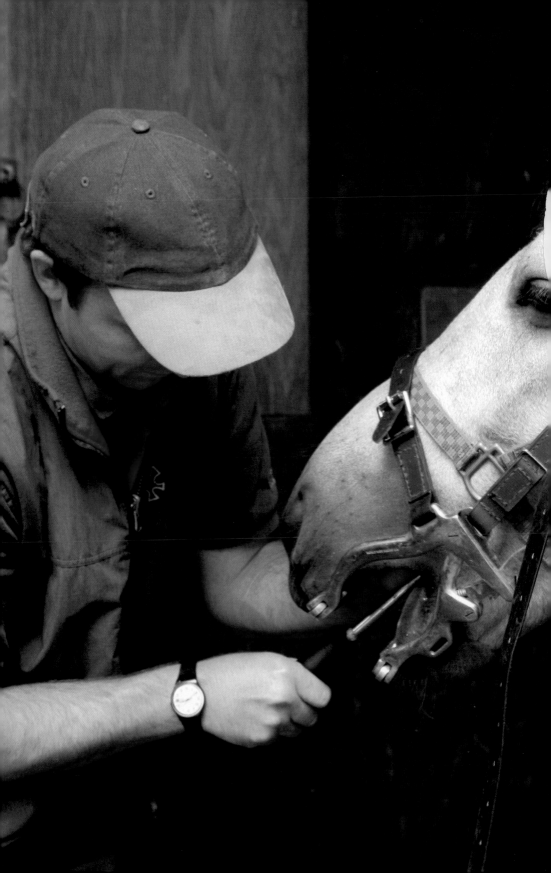

2. Comfort First

Routine dental checks and, when necessary, treatment by a good equine vet or a British Equine Veterinary Association-qualified equine dental technician (EDT) should be part of every horse or pony's management, whether the animal is in work or retired. This will ensure that he can eat properly and, in the case of the ridden or driven animal, will help to ensure that he is comfortable wearing a bit and receiving signals through it.

Take your vet or dentist's advice about how often your horse should be checked. In many cases, once a year will be adequate but some horses need seeing more frequently. For instance, young horses who haven't got their full set of adult teeth—usually in place by the end of their fifth year—may need checking every six months.

If you notice any problems in between scheduled visits, get your horse checked rather than waiting until your appointment is due. Things to watch out for include quidding, where the horse drops food as he eats, or any resistance which could be related to mouth problems. This includes throwing his head up and down, setting his jaw against the rein aids or sticking his tongue over the bit or out the side of his mouth.

Common sense tells you that there may be other things to check first. For instance, if you buy a new bridle or a new bit and a horse suddenly starts putting his tongue over the mouthpiece or holds it out of the side of his mouth, check the relevant sizes and adjustments, as explained later in this chapter.

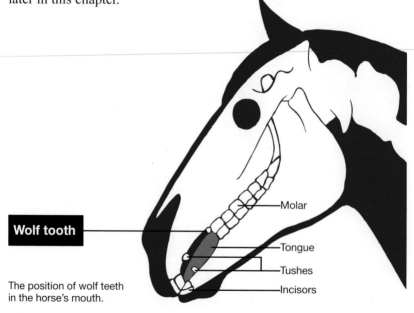

Wolf tooth

Molar

Tongue

Tushes

Incisors

The position of wolf teeth in the horse's mouth.

Also, tongue resistances are sometimes indicators of stress. If a horse does not understand his work, or is being asked to work in a way that he is not yet ready for, poking out his tongue or trying to put it over the bit may be a signal that he can't cope.

Sharp edges on the cheek teeth are one of the commonest causes of mouth discomfort. Horses' teeth, unlike ours, grow at around 2–3mm (0.08–0.12in) per year for most of their lives. Domesticated horses rarely graze fibrous material for long enough periods to ensure that the wear rate matches the growth rate.

When the grinding pattern becomes uneven, sharp edges rub or cut the insides of the cheeks. Some horses may also have teeth which are not in ideal alignment, either because of mouth conformation or perhaps because a tooth has been lost or damaged. Rasping the teeth (called floating in the USA) restores a correct grinding pattern.

Wolf teeth, which are shallow-rooted, vestigial molars, sometimes cause problems by coming into contact with the bit. At one time, it was standard practice to remove them, but some experts now believe that unless a horse is showing signs of discomfort, it is better to leave wolf teeth alone. Talk to your vet or EDT about your particular horse.

Some practitioners believe that bit seats, made by rounding the first cheek teeth, help to ensure that the bit lies more comfortably. It's best to discuss this with your vet or EDT, who will explain whether or not this is advisable for your horse.

Troubleshooting

Rasping should not cause any pain and if a horse resists, it is probably because he is nervous at being restrained or worried about having the rasp in his mouth and/or the noise and vibration which result. An experienced vet or EDT will usually be able to give a horse confidence, but in some cases it is easier and safer if the horse is given a mild sedative whilst the procedure is carried out. Only a vet can administer a sedative or carry out any procedure classed as surgery. In these circumstances, you need to either ask your vet to carry out the dental procedure or arrange for a vet to sedate the horse so that an EDT can rasp the animal's teeth.

Examining a Horse's Mouth

A vet or EDT will use a device called a gag to make a thorough examination of a horse's mouth. This holds the horse's jaws open, without causing him any discomfort, so the back of the mouth can be seen and treated. Just as important, it means there is no risk of the horse closing his mouth on a vulnerable hand or finger!

Raising the lips gently will allow you to inspect the gums and inside of the lips and tickling the tongue or pressing down on the bars of the mouth will encourage the horse to open his mouth and, probably, stick out his tongue. This will help you assess his mouth conformation and perhaps spot signs of ulcers, rubs or nicks.

Some people may advise you to hold the horse's tongue and pull it through the side of the horse's mouth. Don't do this unless your vet recommends you do so and shows you a safe technique. Not only could you get bitten—because again, a horse could close his mouth without being in any way aggressive—you could damage the tongue.

Check the corners of the lips for rubs or splits. If you find anything, don't put a bit in the horse's mouth until the damage has healed and check everything from the condition of your bit to its size and adjustment in the mouth.

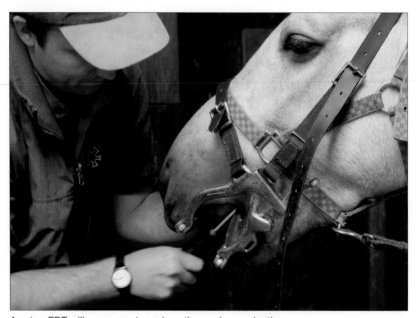

A vet or EDT will use a gag to make a thorough examination.

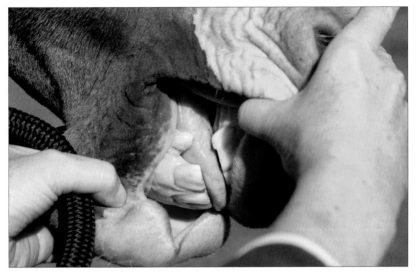

Raise the lips gently to make sure they and the gums are in good condition.

Some horses are more sensitive than others. If there is nothing wrong with the bit, try using a little petroleum jelly on the corners of the mouth to prevent friction.

If you are riding a four- or five-year-old, his adult teeth will be displacing juvenile ones. Some horses seem to be unaffected by this, but others show signs of discomfort. Be patient and, if necessary, get advice on whether to give him a short break or, if appropriate, work him without a bit—either by concentrating on ground work or using a bitless bridle if appropriate. *See* Chapter 8 for more information.

Examining Bits

Is the bit you're using or intend to use well made and in good condition? This is something even experienced riders sometimes forget to check.

Well-made bits aren't the cheapest, but they are the best investment. Faults to look out for include rough edges round the holes of loose ring snaffles and bits which allow more play on one cheek than the other.

Some materials, such as rubber and plastics, suit some horses but may be damaged by a horse's teeth even when they are of good quality. They should always have a metal core to ensure that the horse can't bite through them and leave the rider with no control. If a horse chews such a bit and causes rough areas which could rub the mouth, the bit must be replaced.

A horse's teeth can damage even a good quality bit.

Some metals are more hard-wearing than others. For instance, copper—which is said to encourage a horse to salivate—is softer than stainless steel. Bit manufacturers now tend to use copper in conjunction with other materials rather than on its own to avoid this problem.

However, you may still find mouthpieces which include plain copper lozenges or rollers. It's better to use an alloy which contains copper and these are available under a variety of brand names.

There is more information about materials and their uses in Chapter 4.

Before you consider different bit designs, you need to think about where a bit lies and how it acts. You also need to assess the shape of your horse's mouth, inside and out. This will affect the design and

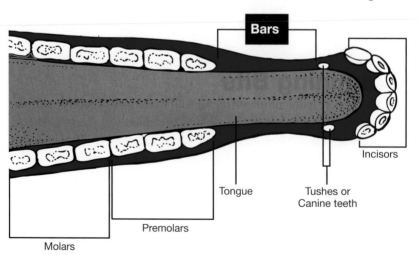

A bit rests on the bars of the mouth.

width of the mouthpiece you use and help you make sure the bit is adjusted correctly.

A bit lies across the tongue and rests on the bars of the mouth; the bars are the space between the last corner incisor and the first premolar. Through the rein aids, pressure is applied via the tongue, the bars of the mouth and the corners of the lips.

Some bits, depending on their design, also act on the poll and the curb groove. A bit should never act on the roof of the mouth, even if it has a port (arch) in the centre of the mouthpiece.

Different breeds and types may have common characteristics, but they aren't guaranteed. For instance, whilst many Arabs and Arab crosses have dished faces and low palates, some are easier to bit than others.

Look at your horse's overall conformation, too, as this will influence his natural way of going. A horse who is 'born on the bit' should find it easier to work correctly than one who does not have perfect conformation.

That doesn't mean that a horse who, for instance, has a shorter, thicker neck than ideal can't work beautifully. He can, especially if he has a good, trainable temperament. The Pony Club's book, *So You Want to Buy a Pony?* gives more information on conformation in general.

Some – but not all – Arabs have low palates.

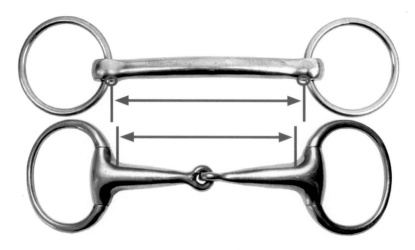

How to measure the length of a loose ring and eggbutt snaffle. With a loose ring bit, take the measurement from the edge of the ring closest to the mouth on each side.

Shaping Up

Choosing the right bit is a matter of choosing the ideal combination of mouthpiece and cheekpiece. Assessing your horse's mouth conformation will help you do that.

From the outside, does your horse have fleshy lips? This is a common characteristic of cobs and other animals with draught or heavy horse blood and means you have to be careful that the bit is at the correct height in the horse's mouth, as explained later in this chapter.

You need to know how much room a horse has in his mouth so that you can choose a mouthpiece which is comfortable for him. When your horse is relaxed, gently move his lips to see how much room his tongue takes up in his mouth. If he has a fat tongue, you will need a mouthpiece which accommodates this, as explained in Chapter 4.

Some horses' mouths are relatively short from the corners of the lips to the end of the muzzle. Again, this means you need to think about mouthpiece design so you use a bit which rests correctly on the tongue. The centre of a single-jointed bit may sit too low, but a double-jointed or mullen mouth bit should rest in the correct place.

Look at the bars of his mouth. Are they fairly wide, with a good covering of flesh, or do they seem narrower, with a sharper edge? Narrow bars mean that the bit is in contact with a smaller bearing surface, so may be an indicator that a horse will react better to a thicker mouthpiece.

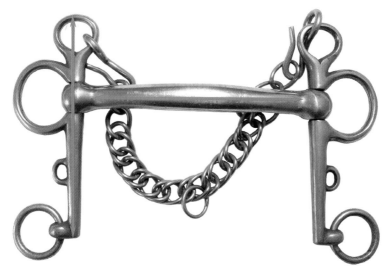

How to measure the length of a pelham mouthpiece and cheeks.

Sizing It Up

Whatever type of bit you use, it must be the right size for your horse's mouth. All horses and ponies should be looked at as individuals—you can't assume that the larger the horse, the larger the bit he will need. Some large horses with small muzzles need small bits and conversely, some ponies need larger bits than you might imagine would be the case.

The length of a bit mouthpiece is measured as shown on the previous page and manufacturers give measurements in inches, centimetres or millimetres. The thickness of a mouthpiece is taken as the diameter of the widest part, near the cheeks or rings.

Pelhams and curbs are available in a choice of cheek lengths. The cheeks are usually measured from top to bottom and the standard proportion is that the cheek is the same length as the mouthpiece. English-style riders only use curbs as part of a double bridle, which is explained later.

If you know that your horse's current bit fits well, this will give you a size basis to work on if you decide to try another one. However, you'll still need to check the fit when it's in the horse's mouth, as design factors affect the way a bit lies in the mouth.

Whatever mouthpiece you use, it must be long enough to prevent the horse's lips being pinched, but not so long that it slides from side to side. The commonest mistake is to use a bit that is too long. This means that it will not lie correctly in the horse's mouth and, especially if it is jointed, it will lie off-centre and too low on the tongue.

As a result, it will irritate the horse and he may put his tongue over the bit. Once this happens, the bit will be uncomfortable or even painful and the horse will react accordingly.

If a mouthpiece is too short, it will pinch the corners of the mouth and the inside of the lips will be pressed against the horse's teeth. If you use a loose ring bit, be extra careful: you don't want the bit to sit too low in the mouth, but you also need to check that his lips can't be pinched between the loose ring and the hole.

To see whether a jointed bit is the correct size, you need to straighten it gently in the horse's mouth. When you hold a loose ring snaffle in the correct position, there should be no more than 1cm (0.4in) between the hole on each side and the horse's lips. A bit with fixed cheeks, such as an eggbutt snaffle, can fit more closely, but again, it must not pinch the lips.

An unjointed bit should fit snugly into the corners of the mouth without pinching and not be so large that it slides from side to side and bangs against the sides of the horse's face. Remember that a horse's muzzle is wider above his lips than below it, so you need to check that the upper cheeks of a full cheek or Fulmer snaffle, or of a pelham or curb, are not pressing in to his face.

The Right Height

As well as being the right size, a bit must be adjusted so that it fits at the correct height in a horse's mouth. This is where your assessment of his mouth conformation will help.

The theory that you should adjust a bit so that there are a certain number of wrinkles in a horse's lips doesn't work. Fleshy lips wrinkle more easily than taut ones and if you are aiming for, say, two wrinkles on each side you could find that a bit is still too low or too high.

Instead, adjust the bit so that it fits snugly into the corners of your horse's mouth and let him get used to the feel of it. Then, ask him to open his mouth and look where the mouthpiece lies. It should lie comfortably across the bars and tongue without coming into contact with his canine teeth—which are usually seen only in geldings, but are also found in a very small percentage of mares. If the mouthpiece has a single joint, it should be positioned over the centre of the tongue. The same applies to the lozenge or plate of a double-jointed mouthpiece.

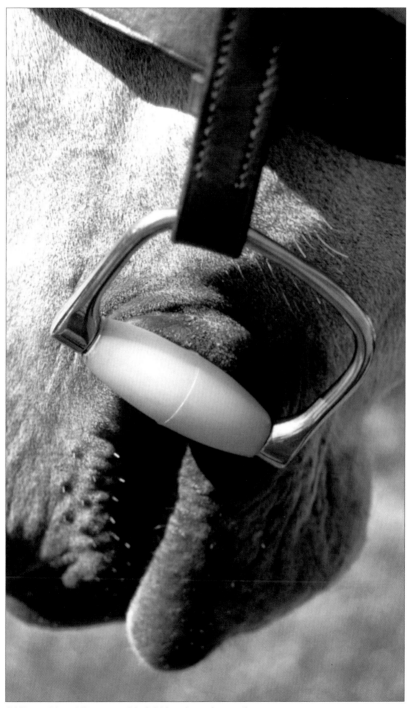

A bit must be at the correct height in a horse's mouth.

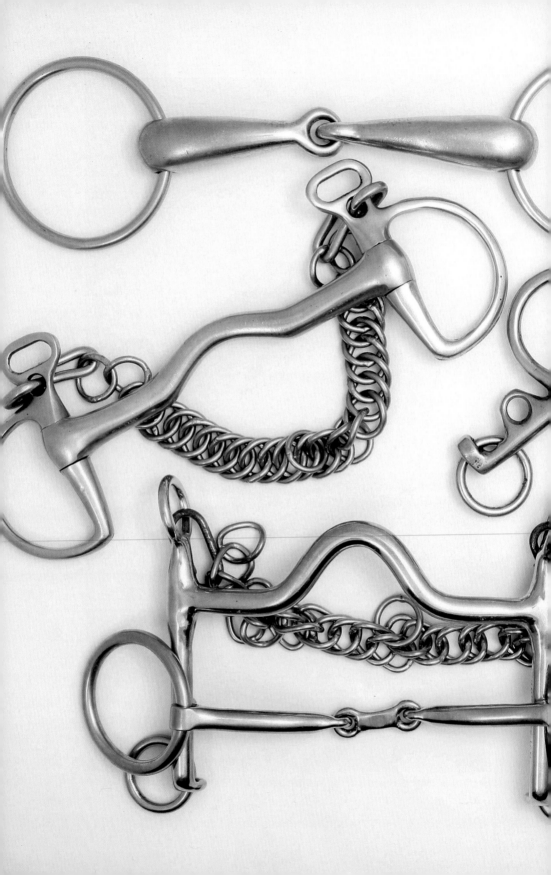

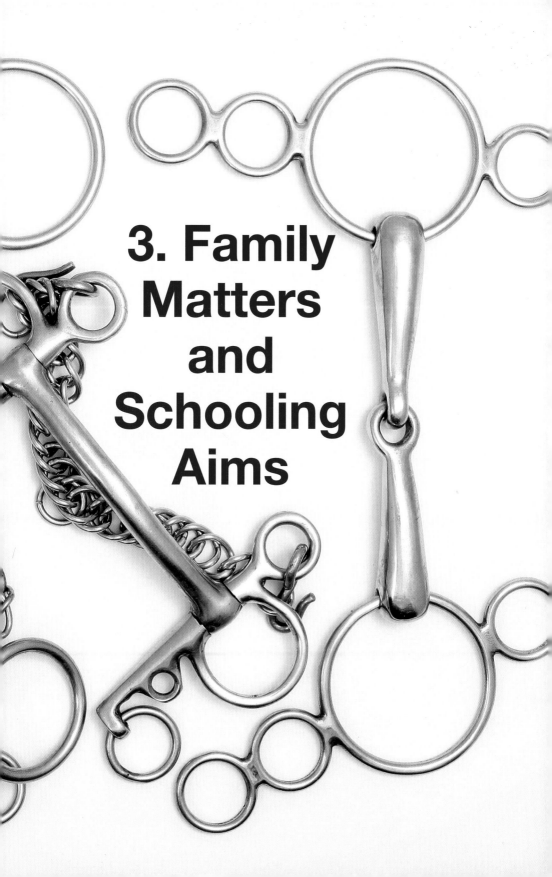

3. Family Matters and Schooling Aims

The huge variety of bits available runs into thousands of designs. Some have been used for many years whilst others have been developed more recently.

Bits can be divided into groups, or families. Traditionally, these groups are snaffles; double bridles; pelhams (which also includes Kimblewicks) and gag snaffles. Bitless bridles form another group even though they obviously do not act on the mouth. As more designs have appeared, we needed to add two more bit groups—lever snaffles, which apply pressure on the poll as well as the mouth, and combination bits, which act on the nose as well as on the mouth.

Bits can act on a variety of control points. All work to some extent on the lips and corners of the mouth, the bars and the tongue. Depending on the design, a bit may apply enough leverage to apply pressure on the poll via the bridle headpiece and, if a curb chain is fitted, in the curb groove—which is sometimes called the chin groove.

There may be times when you need or want to use a bitless bridle. Even if this doesn't arise, understanding various designs and how they work adds to your overall knowledge.

The Bit Families

You'll find detailed information about different designs throughout this book, but first, here is a brief look at the different families of bits.

If you ask any rider to name the simplest and kindest form of bit, the answer will inevitably be a **snaffle.** With most designs, especially those which are permitted for dressage competitions—and which are referred to in this book as simple snaffles—this is true. A simple snaffle is the best bit for a novice rider and a young horse and in some cases, may be the only bit you will ever need for a particular horse.

The **double bridle** comprises two bits, each operated independently. One is a bradoon, which is a snaffle with a thin mouthpiece and small rings. The other is a curb, which as well as acting on the mouth, applies pressure on the poll and, via the curb chain, on the curb groove at the back of the horse's jaw. A double bridle allows very subtle communication and is suitable only for experienced, competent riders.

The **pelham** was originally designed to try and combine the actions of the double bridle in a single mouthpiece. It can't actually do that, but it is still a useful bit that many horses find comfortable and many riders

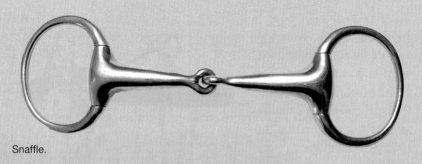

Snaffle.

Pelham.

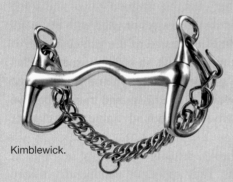

Kimblewick.

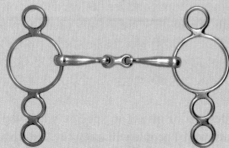

Lever snaffle.

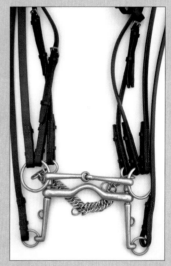

Double bridle.

Gag snaffle.

are happy with. It has a curb chain and can be used with two pairs of reins, or with a single rein and leather couplings which join the top and bottom bit rings on each side.

Combination bit.

The **Kimblewick** belongs to the pelham family and is named after the village in which its designer lived. It has a single ring, so is used with one rein. Although it has a curb chain, this hardly comes into effect because the bit rings apply very little leverage to move the curb chain against the curb groove.

The **gag snaffle** was designed to give control over strong horses in exciting situations, such as cross country. It is used with special cheekpieces that run through holes in the top and bottom of the bit rings. It is potentially severe, but effective in good hands and some event riders still use it. Ideally, it should always be used with two pairs of reins—one attached to the rings at the end of the gag cheekpieces and the other direct to the bit rings, as with an ordinary snaffle. This allows the rider to employ the gag action only when needed, which protects the horse's mouth. However, some riders and trainers believe that riding cross country with two reins is not advisable—*see* chapter 4 for more information.

Lever snaffles have long cheeks, usually with slots or rings at different heights to take the reins. They apply poll and mouth pressure and the lower the rein position, the greater the potential pressure.

Combination bits have built-in nosebands and are designed to act on the nose as well as on the mouth. Again, they are usually used to give extra control.

Rider Position

Although different types and designs of bit act in specific ways, the rider has a huge effect. For a start, whilst people will often say that a bit is 'mild' or 'severe' it isn't as simple as that. A bit's action depends on

A rider in a balanced, effective position.

the way a rider uses it and the simplest design can be potentially severe if the rider is uncoordinated or rough.

So whilst this book isn't a riding manual, it's appropriate to offer a few reminders about rider position and the use of the reins. Your instructor should be able to explain farther.

A good rider has a balanced seat and does not rely on the reins for security. Good hands can only begin with good balance! The classically-correct riding position isn't just someone's idea of what looks elegant: it allows you to sit in a way that makes it easier to absorb the horse's movement, doesn't interfere with the way he moves and balances himself and allows you to apply the aids clearly, without force.

As part of that balanced seat, think about how you connect to the horse through the reins. Here are some pointers you should try and remember.

- Allow your shoulders to drop so they are level, but not forced back, or rounded.
- Allow your elbows to rest lightly at your side.
- Bend your elbows softly so that the muscles in your arms—particularly those in the lower arm—are soft. If your arms are straight, without a bend in your elbows, the muscles will be tight and you will lose sensitivity.
- Your wrists should be *very* slightly rounded to the inside, not bent to the outside or held as if you were pushing a bicycle.

The usual method of holding a single pair of reins is for the rein to pass between the ring finger and little finger, with fingers closed round it without gripping tightly.

- When holding a single pair of reins, as with a snaffle bridle, the rein should pass between the ring finger and little finger. Think about holding it securely between your thumb and first finger, then close your fingers round it without gripping tightly. However, don't ride with open fingers—a lot of people do, because they think that this makes their rein contact more sensitive. Actually, it does the opposite.
- For more information on using two pairs of reins, with either a double bridle or a pelham, *see* page 57.

The Way Bits Work

It's often said that some bits act to raise a horse's head when the rein aids are applied and that others act to lower it, but this is an over simplified and therefore not always accurate explanation. Bit actions vary according to the horse's stage of training and the way he carries himself.

Of course, the rider also has an effect, as lowering or raising the hands and arms—whether deliberately or without realising that you are doing so—will lower or raise the bit in the horse's mouth. This is why the principles of developing an independent seat and keeping a correct arm and hand position are so important, as this will affect the feel you establish through the reins.

A young horse who is just starting his ridden education, or an older one who has only had very basic training, will carry more weight on his forehand even if he isn't heavy in the rider's hand. When he's ridden and the rider has a light contact on the reins, this horse's face will be in front of the vertical. As such, the rider's hands, and therefore the bit, will act in an upward direction and any pressure will be more on the corners of the mouth than on the bars.

As the horse's schooling improves, he will lift his abdominal muscles and engage his hindlegs. This will, in turn, mean that he comes off his forehand and distributes his weight more evenly, pushing himself from behind rather than pulling himself along from his shoulders and front legs.

At the same time, he will arch his neck slightly and his face will come on the vertical. You have to accept that until a horse is fully established in his training—and unless he is ridden correctly—his head carriage will vary as he finds his balance. There will always be times when even a well-schooled horse comes slightly in front of or slightly behind the vertical, but it should not be an exaggerated fault.

On and Off the Bit

When you first start riding, you learn to start, stop and steer whilst keeping a light contact with the horse or pony's mouth. As you progress, you will learn to influence the horse's way of going so that he uses the whole of his body in balance and can change pace—including variations within a pace, for example from working trot to collected trot—and direction effortlessly and smoothly.

In English-style riding, this requires a horse to be 'on the bit.' A Western-style rider can also have a horse in perfect balance, but because of the difference in the styles of riding and in the type of bits used, a Western-style rider will have a looser rein and the horse will have a lower head carriage, though this doesn't mean he will be on his forehand.

Because we'll be talking about how you can choose bits to try and encourage your horse to go in a particular way, let's have some definitions.

The FEI—the governing body for international equestrian sport—says that 'on the bit' means that the horse's hocks are correctly placed and that his neck is raised and arched according to the stage of training and the extension or collection of the pace. He should accept the bridle with a light, soft contact and his head should remain steady, usually slightly

Western-style riders adopt a longer rein and their horses go with a lower head carriage.

in front of the vertical, with a supple poll as the highest part of the neck.

Your instructor will explain this if necessary, but even though this is the ideal that all riders aim for, even top dressage riders don't always achieve it! For instance, whilst a horse can be in balance and fulfil the other criteria of being on the bit, his natural conformation may mean that the poll is not always the highest point.

Unfortunately, the phrase 'on the bit' can trap us into focussing on the horse's head and neck rather than thinking of his whole body coming into self carriage. One of the commonest mistakes is to concentrate on asking the horse to bring in his head and neck, without asking him to lift his abdominal muscles and use his hindlegs.

For a horse or pony to work on the bit, he must have the muscular development which comes through a correct work programme. This comes more easily to horses who have textbook conformation than to those who don't, but with time and patience, every horse can be schooled to work correctly.

He also has to be able to adjust his centre of gravity so that he is pushing from his back end rather than pulling from his front end. Researchers say that most of the time, a horse naturally takes 60 per cent of his weight on his forehand; add the weight of a rider and it's easy to see why it takes time for him to develop the strength and suppleness to lighten his forehand.

However, watch any horse playing or showing off to others out in the field and you'll see that on his own, he is quite capable of showing fantastic balance and paces, whether he is a cob, a pony or a horse specifically bred for dressage. We're the ones who cause the problems, so we have to learn how to ride and school him so he can regain that natural balance whilst carrying a rider!

A horse may also be above the bit or behind the bit, neither of which is desirable. Both are resistances and may occur momentarily or for a longer period.

When a horse comes above the bit, he raises his head and neck, which causes tension throughout his body and means he can't use himself correctly. When he comes behind the bit, he backs off from taking a comfortable contact and again, will not use his body correctly.

Don't worry if you haven't reached a stage in your riding where you can school a horse or pony. You'll get there, but in the meantime, it helps to have something to aim for!

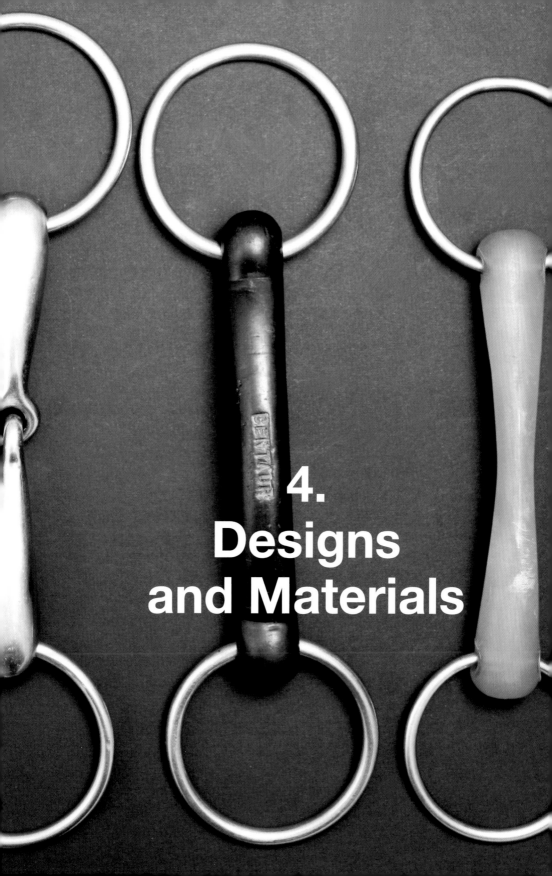

4.
Designs
and Materials

Bits are made with a huge variety of mouthpieces and cheekpieces and finding the right combination will help you get the best results from your horse. You need to think about the design of the bit, the material it is made from and also the thickness of the mouthpiece.

A horse with a very wet mouth.

In theory, a thicker mouthpiece is milder than a thinner one because it has a greater bearing area. In practice, some horses don't have room in their mouths for a thick mouthpiece, often because they have a fat, fleshy tongue.

A horse needs to have a reasonably wet mouth when ridden, though this doesn't mean that there needs to be foam round his lips. If his mouth is dry, the bit will drag over his tongue and bars rather than slide. He will only have a wet mouth if he can close it round the bit, which he will be unable to do if it is literally too much of a mouthful.

To make things simple, this chapter starts by looking at snaffle mouthpieces. This information also applies to bradoons, which, as well as being one half of a double bridle, can also be used alone for horses who don't have room in their mouths for a thick mouthpiece, or who go better with a thinner bit even if they could accommodate a thicker one.

Unjointed Mouthpieces

There are two types of unjointed mouthpiece: the straight bar and the mullen or half moon. The latter, as its name suggests, has a slight arch throughout its length.

A straight bar mouthpiece does not allow any room for a horse's tongue, so applies more tongue pressure. Many horses dislike this.

The exception is a bit constructed as a straight bar, but made from flexible material, as this makes a slight curve when a contact is taken on the reins. *See* the Material World section later in this chapter.

Although a mullen mouthpiece gives some tongue pressure, it is not as pronounced and many horses go kindly in it. It doesn't drop down in the centre as a jointed bit will, so is often useful for horses who are fussy in the mouth or who try and put their tongue over the bit. A mullen mouth bit can be fitted high enough to prevent the horse doing this without pulling the corners of his lips too high, so it is more comfortable.

Single-jointed Mouthpiece

The traditional single-jointed snaffle is one of the oldest designs of bit. There are Iron Age bits on display in museums to which today's snaffles bear a marked resemblance.

At one time, single-jointed snaffles were used more frequently than any other kind. Whilst there is nothing wrong with them, and many horses and ponies go well in them, others go better in a bit which has more than one joint. This is probably because although a single joint allows room for the tongue, it also has a squeezing action. This is more pronounced if the arms of the mouthpiece are straight than if they are shaped with a slight curve.

There are now single-jointed bits available where both the arms and the joint itself are angled slightly. These designs are said to prevent the bit having a squeezing action.

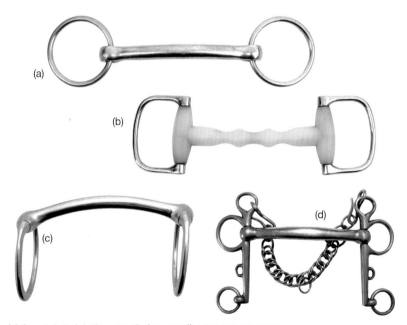

(a) A metal straight bar mouthpiece applies tongue pressure but (b) a flexible straight bar adapts to a slight curve.
(c) and (d) Many horses go kindly in a mullen mouthpiece.

Double-jointed and Multi-jointed Mouthpieces

Double- or multi-jointed mouthpieces still apply tongue pressure, but many horses seem to find them more comfortable. This is probably because they eliminate the squeezing action of the single-jointed mouthpiece.

A double-jointed mouthpiece may have either a lozenge or a shaped central plate. Some manufacturers claim that the angle at which the lozenge is set, combined with the curvature of the arms on either side, makes a difference to its action because it affects the amount of tongue pressure applied.

Lozenge mouthpieces have become more popular than the traditional French link snaffle, called a dogbone snaffle in the USA. The second name is perhaps more accurate, as it describes the shape of the central plate.

Don't confuse the **French link** snaffle with the Dr Bristol. This also has a central plate, but the sides are straight rather than curved and it puts pressure on the tongue rather than relieving it. This is why French link and lozenge snaffles are permitted for dressage, but the **Dr Bristol** isn't.

Bits come into and go out of fashion, often because well-known riders use them. The multi-jointed or **Waterford** snaffle is one that has come back into fashion. Sometimes called a bobble bit, it is completely flexible and follows the shape of a horse's mouth.

The Waterford is traditionally a bit for strong horses, but the reason it is effective may be that a horse finds it comfortable—providing, that is, a rider uses it tactfully and doesn't move it from side to side in the horse's mouth. You can't stop a horse pulling by inflicting discomfort or pain, nor will doing so teach him to 'respect the bit.'

Roller Mouthpieces

Snaffles (and occasionally, pelhams) with rollers around the mouthpiece are sometimes described as suitable for horses which pull or try and lean on the rider's hands. They may help to break the cycle, but the reason is that the mobility of the rollers helps stop the horse setting himself against the rider's hands and encourages him to relax his jaw.

It also—and this is just as important—helps prevent the rider's hands being set against the horse! As the old saying goes, it takes two to pull.

Although they are no longer popular, you might come across a **Magenis** snaffle. This has a square-sided mouthpiece with rollers set inside it.

Single-jointed snaffle.

Snaffle with a central lozenge.

French link snaffle.

Dr Bristol snaffle.

Waterford snaffle.

A snaffle with rollers set round the mouthpiece is potentially less harsh than the Magenis snaffle, which has rollers set inside.

Because the sides are flat, they apply definite pressure or even dig into the tongue. For this reason, it can't be recommended under any circumstances.

The downside of roller snaffles is that they are usually made with straight mouthpiece arms, which gives a definite squeezing action. You also need to check that they are well made and that there is no chance that the horse's tongue can be pinched. This can happen with snaffles which incorporate stainless steel and copper rollers, as copper is softer and wears more quickly.

(a)

(b)

The square sides of the Magenis snaffle (a) add to its potential severity. When copper rollers alternate with metal ones (b), the softer copper wears more quickly.

This Myler mouthpiece is said to follow the contours of the mouth.

Myler Snaffles

The Myler range of bits includes designs which are often confused with roller snaffles, which is why it is referred to in this book by name. Mouthpieces are curved to follow the shape of the mouth—a feature also found in other ranges—and most have barrels covering the joints. This means that there is no squeezing action.

Some of the snaffles are also available with two slots in each cheek, which the American designers refer to as hooks. The slots take the bridle cheekpieces and reins and act to stabilise the bit in the mouth and add slight poll pressure. Snaffles with slots are currently not permitted for dressage under either Pony Club or British Dressage rules.

Myler snaffles are said to have independent side action, as each side pivots on the barrel. As with any bit, they work well for some horse and rider combinations but not for others—and, as always, this may be related to the rider as well as, or rather than, the horse!

Material World

The material from which a mouthpiece is made can make a big difference to the way a horse accepts it—or not! As explained earlier, you need a horse to relax his jaw and have a reasonably wet mouth and whilst achieving this comes mainly from balance and lack of tension, materials which encourage salivation may help in some cases.

Don't confuse the wet mouth of a relaxed horse with that of one who chomps and chews excessively on the bit. Flying foam is often a sign that a horse is tense or uncomfortable, though admittedly there are also horses who are perfectly happy and relaxed but start slobbering as soon as you take up the reins.

Stainless steel is a traditional material for bits and has the advantage of being easy to clean and hard wearing. In many cases, horses find it perfectly acceptable.

Copper alloys are marketed under a variety of names. They are designed to encourage salivation and, as such, may be useful for horses who seem to need encouragement to mouth the bit.

Some stainless steel mouthpieces incorporate copper or copper alloy lozenges. As explained above, copper is a relatively soft metal and there may be problems with wear when it is used alone.

When copper alloy bits are new, they are an attractive gold colour. In use, they become dull. This doesn't detract from their effectiveness, but you can buy special cleaners if you want to restore their sparkling appearance.

Sweet iron mouthpieces originated in America and are also designed to encourage a horse to salivate. Manufacturers often say that they oxidise, which is the same as saying that they rust, but sounds better!

This in itself isn't a problem and is a clever way of re-inventing the wheel. Before the invention of stainless steel, dealers and nagsmen used their oldest, rustiest bits when starting off young horses for riding and driving because they found that horses accepted them more easily.

Some manufacturers advise that if a sweet iron bit isn't in regular use, the mouthpiece should be coated with cooking oil before storage.

Rubber mouthpieces are used in jointed and unjointed bits and are popular with some riders because they think of them as 'kind.' The rubber can be soft or treated so it hardens and the rubber can be used either as a coating for a metal bit, which will give the bit rigidity, or over a thin, bendy core, in which case the mouthpiece flexes. Some horses like rubber bits, but they are easily damaged by horses' teeth and can be heavy and bulky.

Vulcanised rubber bits, often referred to as vulcanite, are harder and are also bulky. They are still available, but generally not as popular as ordinary hardened rubber ones.

Nylon mouthpieces are more resistant than rubber to wear and tear and are also lighter in weight. The commonest nylon bits are mullen mouth snaffles used for showing horses and ponies in hand, but they are rarely used for riding.

Bits made from lightweight but reasonably strong plastic are often used on young horses and those with sensitive mouths. They can also be damaged by a horse's teeth and, as with rubber bits, should have a metal core, so that they are unlikely to be chewed through.

Plastic mouthpieces range from flexible unjointed ones to those with single joints or a central plastic lozenge.

Copper alloy mouthpiece.

Sweet iron mouthpiece.

Rubber mouthpiece.

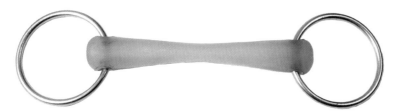

Plastic mouthpiece.

Cheek Options

When you have settled on a snaffle or bradoon mouthpiece that you think would suit your horse, the next part of equation is deciding what type of cheekpiece to use. The ones in common use which can be classed as simple snaffles are the eggbutt, loose ring, Fulmer, full cheek, D-ring and hanging cheek. There is a subtle difference between the Fulmer and full cheek snaffles: the Fulmer has a loose ring set outside the mouthpiece, so allows a little more play, whilst the full cheek is fixed.

The **eggbutt** snaffle stays relatively still in the horse's mouth and the smooth sections at the end of the mouthpiece which give the bit its name prevent the corners of the mouth being pinched. They also mean that the bit stays central in the mouth.

Both factors make it a good choice for a rider who has not yet established an independent seat and who has unsteady hands. This is why it is often used in riding schools. It can also help with a horse who lacks confidence in the bit and tends to come above or behind it.

The **loose ring** snaffle is more mobile in the horse's mouth. It is usually a good choice for a horse who feels 'wooden' in the mouth when ridden in a fixed cheek bit, such as an eggbutt, or who tries to lean on the bit. It isn't a good choice for a rider who has unsteady hands, as it exaggerates the fault.

A possible drawback of the loose ring snaffle is that it can be pulled off-centre in the horse's mouth if a rider unwittingly uses stronger rein aids with one hand. Many of us are stronger with our dominant hand, without realising it—so if you are right handed, you may take a stronger contact on the right rein.

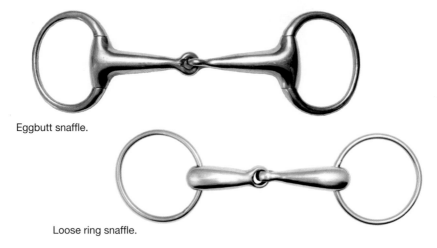

Eggbutt snaffle.

Loose ring snaffle.

Riding with your stronger hand underneath the rein helps avoid tension.

If you think this might be the case, you could try riding with your stronger hand underneath the rein rather than on top. This relaxes the muscles in your lower arm and you may find that your horse suddenly goes much better! Once you know what an even hold on the reins feels like, go back to the correct position.

If you already use a Flash or drop noseband (*see* Chapter 7) it will help to keep the bit central. If you use a plain cavesson noseband, use a pair of rubber bitguards instead. Unfortunately, these are not allowed in dressage competitions.

A **sleeve** or **T-bar** snaffle offers the mobility of a loose ring snaffle with the comfort factor of the eggbutt one. As the names suggest, the loose ring runs through a T-shaped sleeve, which prevents any pinching. It also helps to keep the bit central in the mouth.

Sleeve or T-bar snaffle.

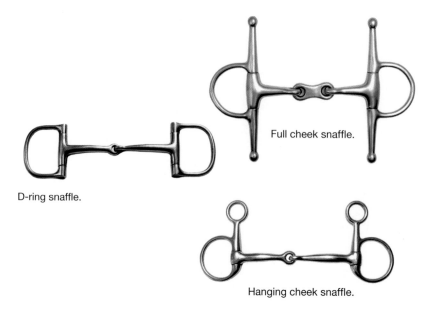

Full cheek snaffle.

D-ring snaffle.

Hanging cheek snaffle.

A **full cheek** snaffle stays central in the horse's mouth and applies slight pressure to the sides of the horse's face. This helps to reinforce steering and makes it a popular bit for young horses starting out on their education. Because it is a fixed bit, it stays relatively still in the horse's mouth. If you want to keep the full cheeks but add a little more mobility, use either a full cheek snaffle with a lozenge or French link mouthpiece or try a Fulmer snaffle, where the loose rings add a little play.

A **Fulmer** snaffle should always be used with leather keepers which attach the bit cheeks to the bridle cheekpieces. If you try and use it without these, the cheeks will be at the wrong angle and steering reinforcement will be lost.

Keepers have the effect of minimising tongue pressure slightly and ensuring that the central joint or joints remain high enough in the mouth. If your horse has short lips, this can make it easier to adjusts the bit at the correct height without pulling the corners of the mouth too high.

If your horse has a wide muzzle, as is the case with many cobs and heavier native breeds, be careful that the top part of a full cheek or Fulmer snaffle doesn't dig into his face. Some designs have the top cheeks angled slightly away from the face to take this possibility into account, but unfortunately this is no longer a standard design feature, and you may need to shop around for a bit which your horse will find comfortable.

You may also find problems if your horse has a relatively short muzzle and you use a cavesson or Flash noseband. If the noseband is fitted correctly, so that it does not rub against the facial bones, there may not be sufficient space between the top of the bit cheeks and the bottom of the noseband to prevent one or both cheeks becoming caught underneath the noseband. In this case, you could use a **D-ring** snaffle, which also helps with steering, but is not as definite in its action as a full cheek or Fulmer.

Fulmer snaffle with keepers.

There is a slight possibility that a full cheek snaffle can become caught up if, for instance, a horse is allowed to rub his nose on his leg whilst wearing brushing boots. For this reason, a D-ring snaffle may be a safer choice for children's ponies, as young riders are unlikely to be as aware or quick to react as adults.

Hanging cheek snaffles apply a little poll pressure, which some horses respond well to and others dislike. They also relieve pressure on the tongue, as they are suspended in the mouth. Most riders use them to encourage a horse to lower its head and assume a rounder outline, but unless the horse is ridden correctly there is a danger that he will set his head and neck rather than working from behind into a soft contact.

Gag, Lever and Loop Snaffles

Whilst many readers of this book will never need or want to use a gag or lever snaffle, others may consider doing so. Loop snaffles—bits marketed under various names which have loops inside the main rings to take the bridle cheekpieces and reins—are included because they have become popular in the show ring. Both lever and loop snaffles are sometimes mistakenly referred to as having a similar action to a gag snaffle, but this is not the case.

The Real Thing

The true **gag snaffle** is designed to give more control over a horse who becomes strong in certain situations, such as when going cross country. It is also a favourite bit of many polo players, though some use it with more finesse than others.

A gag snaffle has special cheekpieces made from rolled leather or rope. These run through slots at the top and bottom of the bit rings, which can be eggbutt, loose ring or even full cheek. Rolled leather cheeks which are kept clean and supple tend to run more smoothly than rope ones.

This bit is designed for use with two pairs of reins. One pair attaches to the rings at the end of the gag cheekpieces and the other direct to the bit rings, as with an ordinary snaffle.

This allows the rider to employ the gag action only when needed, which protects the horse's mouth. The reins are held and manipulated in the same way as the reins of a pelham or double bridle, as explained in Chapter 5.

The idea is that for most of the time, the rider employs the direct rein, in which case the bit has the action of an ordinary snaffle. If the horse becomes strong, and especially if he lowers his head to pull, using the gag rein raises the bit in the horse's mouth.

This bit must only be used by a rider who can use the gag rein subtly and release it as soon as the horse answers the action of the bit. If you maintain pressure on the rein, you will hurt your horse's mouth and he will probably pull harder.

Some riders and trainers feel that it is inadvisable to ride cross country with two reins. However, riding with a single gag rein puts constant pressure on the lips and poll and it would be better to look for an alternative bit.

Lever snaffles are bits which, as the name suggests, employ a certain amount of leverage and, therefore, poll pressure. Whilst hanging cheek snaffles, pelhams and Kimblewicks also act on the poll, they do so to a lesser degree.

Lever snaffles have a small ring to take the bridle cheekpieces and rings or slots at intervals down the bit cheeks. They are available with a wide range of mouthpieces.

The lever snaffle in commonest use is the three-ring snaffle. It is often called a three-ring gag, even by manufacturers, but doesn't have a true gag action because the bridle cheekpieces do not run through the bit rings. However, it is potentially severe.

If this bit is used with a single pair of reins on the top, largest bit ring, it has an action similar to that of a hanging cheek snaffle. There is a little more movement of the mouthpiece, as the rings can move round to a limited extent.

If the rein is attached to the next ring down, then greater leverage can be employed. Using the reins on the bottom ring increases the leverage

True gag snaffle.

The Wilkie snaffle is a type of loop snaffle.

still farther and sadly, this is the setting that most riders use. In many cases, a horse will tuck his nose in to try and get away from the action of the bit, leaving the rider with what may feel like a light contact but may actually translate to considerable pressure on the horse's mouth.

What also happens when the reins are fixed to the lowest ring is that a jointed mouthpiece closes and the centre of the joint points upwards and forwards in the mouth. The horse's reaction is often to open his mouth to try and evade the discomfort. Some riders then use a noseband which fastens below as well as above the bit to prevent him doing so.

If you feel you need to use this bit, at least try using the first or second rein settings rather than the lowest one. It's also recommended that you use a strap at the back of the horse's jaw to link the large rings, as this limits the extent to which the central joint can rise.

It's possible to use this bit with two reins, one attached to the top, mildest ring and the other to the second or third. Again, this allows you to ride on the mildest setting and apply and release greater leverage as needed. Some riders use pelham roundings to link the top and bottom rings, which also limits the upwards movement of the central joint.

If you have been using a simple snaffle and switch to a three-ring snaffle, remember that you will need to raise the bridle cheekpieces to achieve a correct fit. If there are not enough holes left for adjustment, you will need to fit shorter cheekpieces.

Loop snaffles employ poll pressure, but are less definite in their action than a hanging cheek snaffle. They are often used in the show ring to encourage a horse or pony to carry its head and neck in a round outline, especially when a child does not have the experience or length of leg to get a pony truly on the bit.

Lever action snaffle with reins on the top ring.

Lever action snaffle with reins on the bottom ring.

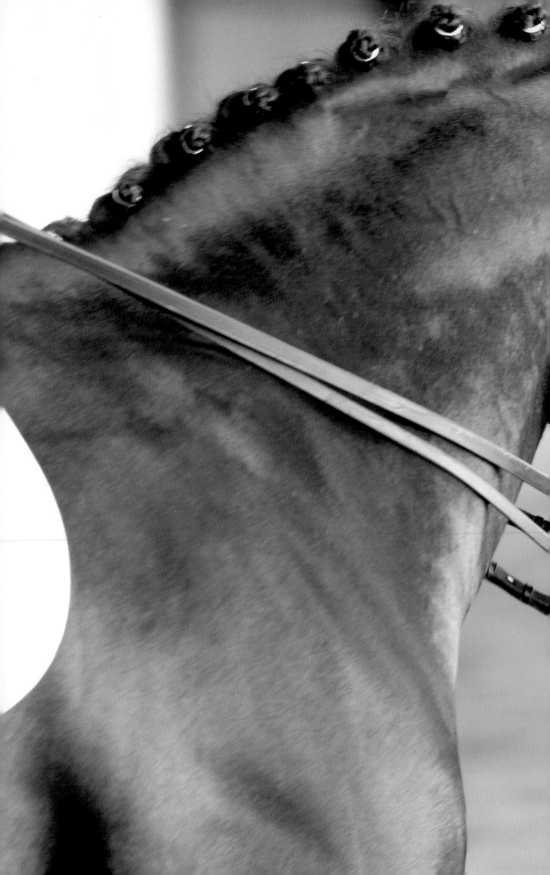

5.
Double Bridles, Pelhams and Kimblewicks

The double bridle, with its two bits, is the most logical and sophisticated bitting arrangement that an educated rider can use on an educated horse. It is not for novices, either two- or four-legged, and it certainly shouldn't be used to try and give extra braking power.

The combination of the bradoon and curb offers the chance of subtle communication, but should be handled with care. A horse must be calm, responsive and working in balance and in self-carriage in a snaffle before a double bridle is introduced and a rider must have an independent seat and knowledge of how a double bridle works before trying to use one.

Because there are two bits, a double bridle has an extra headpiece, called a sliphead. This takes the bradoon, whilst the curb is attached to the ordinary bridle cheekpiece. The sliphead fastens on the offside, purely for the sake of neatness, as you then have the same number of buckles on each side.

As a double bridle is meant to be for an established horse, it is designed to be used with a cavesson noseband, which fastens above the bits and can't interfere with the action of the curb chain. This and a crank noseband, which fastens tighter than an ordinary cavesson one, are the only nosebands permitted for dressage. However, as a horse needs to have a relaxed, mobile jaw to work properly on the bit, fastening a noseband so tightly will often be counterproductive and may cause him discomfort.

You will occasionally see riders using a Grakle noseband with a double bridle, especially when jumping. As with so many things, top riders may have reasons for breaking accepted rules and the ability to do so successfully, but Pony Club teaching remains that a double bridle should only be used with a cavesson noseband.

How It Works

The two bits have different, complementary actions. The bradoon—sometimes called a bridoon, though bradoon is the traditional name—is simply a small snaffle and its action should dominate. The curb, in conjunction with the curb chain, asks the horse to relax his jaw. As he does so, he may bring in his nose and/or lower his head, but this is a secondary action.

In Western-style riding, a curb is often used alone. The reason this is not appropriate for English-style riders is that there is a marked difference in the two styles of riding.

The best Western-style riders are as skilled as their best English-style counterparts and a top Western reining horse that can execute movements such as spins and sliding stops is as well-schooled as a top dressage horse. But Western-style riders rely more on body weight and neck reining—laying the rein against the horse's neck to indicate a turn in direction—than on rein aids which act directly on the horse's mouth.

As such, they should only have to use fingertip pressure on the reins and a horse may be comfortable and happy when a curb bit is used alone. However, you'll find that just as English-style riders carry out a young horse's early training using a snaffle bridle, so Western-

Advanced Western-style riders will use a curb bit on its own.

style trainers will start with either a snaffle or a bitless bridle.

A double bridle is always used with two pairs of reins. At first, it can feel as if you've been presented with too much of a handful—but with a little practice, you'll soon become more confident. It can help to have a lesson or two with a good instructor on an experienced horse who goes nicely in a double bridle. If that isn't possible and you're worried about giving confusing signals, you can always attach two pairs of reins to a snaffle until you are used to manipulating them.

There are several ways of holding double reins, as illustrated in the Pony Club's *Manual of Horsemanship*, but the commonest method is to pass the bradoon rein outside the little finger and the curb rein between the little and fourth (ring) fingers of each hand.

Using this method means that the action of the bradoon rein dominates and all you need to do is close one or both little fingers against your palm to apply an aid. To use the curb rein, close one or both fourth fingers against your palm.

Some riders like to activate the curb rein by turning their hand or hands so their fingernails are upwards, but this can make the muscles in the arm tense. Experiment and see what works best for you.

The commonest method for holding double reins is to pass the bradoon rein outside the little finger and the curb rein between the little and fourth (ring) finger of each hand.

Whilst you should always have an elastic contact through the bradoon rein, the curb rein should be used only when needed. Most of the time, you should be able to hold it so that only the weight of the rein itself acts on the horse's mouth.

In many cases, just the weight of the rein may help encourage the horse to relax his jaw. If the horse consistently overbends and drops behind the contact, the rider is either using too much pressure on the curb rein, or needs to try a combination of bits which give the horse more confidence.

Bit Designs: Bradoons

There are as many types of bradoons as there are snaffles. Curbs are also available in a wide range of designs. This might make it sound as if choosing and fitting a double bridle is twice as complicated as with any other bit, but the same principles apply—you're trying to choose bits which suit the horse's mouth conformation and with which he seems comfortable.

If he goes well in a snaffle with a particular type of mouthpiece, logic suggests that he will accept a bradoon of the same design. For instance, you can use one with a central lozenge.

Most riders use a loose ring bradoon even if they normally ride in a snaffle with fixed cheeks, as the small rings allow less movement than larger ones,

The small rings of a loose ring bradoon allow a little play on the mouthpiece.

but enough to give a little play on the mouthpiece. Some horses who go nicely in a double bridle will go equally nicely in a bradoon on its own for everyday riding, perhaps because they associate it with the feel of a double bridle or even because the rider uses it more tactfully!

If a horse overbends or drops behind the contact and it isn't because you are applying too much pressure on the reins, you may get better results by using an eggbutt bradoon. This, like its snaffle counterpart, stays relatively still in the horse's mouth.

Polo players and even riders in the show ring may sometimes be seen using bradoons that are miniature gag snaffles, with running cheeks going through slots in the rings. If you accept that a double bridle should be used purely to provide a more subtle means of communication, it's difficult to think of any justification for putting such a design in a horse's mouth.

Traditionally, a bradoon has smaller rings than a snaffle. However, some riders and trainers believe that using a bradoon with rings which approximate in size to those of a snaffle allows more definite and direct rein aids. As with so many considerations, the most reliable way to decide whether or not this strategy will be helpful is to see if your horse responds any differently to the different designs.

Bit Designs: Curbs

There are two considerations when choosing a curb: the cheekpiece and the mouthpiece. Cheeks can be sliding or fixed, the difference being that a sliding cheek allows a little movement of the mouthpiece and a fixed cheek remains still. The slight movement of a sliding cheek means the action is less direct than that of a fixed one and some horses simply prefer one to the other.

In general, a sliding cheek is often a good choice for a horse who tends to lean on the bit and a fixed cheek can give confidence to one who comes behind the bit. Logically, a loose ring bradoon is a natural partner for a sliding cheek and an eggbutt one for a fixed cheek, but in practice, many horses go well in a loose ring bradoon whatever type of curb it is paired with.

The length of the curb cheek, both above and below the mouthpiece, will determine the potential leverage. The standard proportions are that the length of the cheekpieces from top to bottom should be the same as the length of the mouthpiece.

Some curbs are made shorter than the bit mouthpiece, which limits the amount of leverage. They are sometimes called Tom Thumb curbs—and if you find yourself being asked to explain this in a quiz, Tom Thumb was a character in a fairy tale who was no bigger than his father's thumb!

The section of the cheek above the mouthpiece is usually designed purely as an attachment point for the bridle cheekpieces. If a manufacturer adds extra length to this section, it will increase the overall leverage.

The shape of a curb mouthpiece can have a big effect on your horse's comfort. Most have some type of port—an arch in the centre of the mouthpiece—which is designed not to put pressure on the roof of the mouth but to take pressure off the centre of the tongue.

Having said that, a curb with a very high port may come into contact with the roof of the mouth. The only place for a bit which does this is in a display case!

If your horse has a fleshy tongue and/or a low palate, you may find that he is most comfortable with a port that is angled slightly forwards.

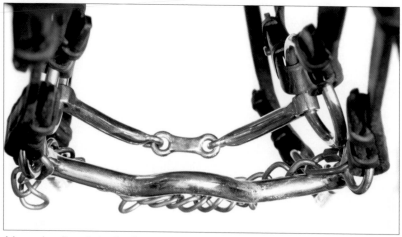

A loose ring, French ring bradoon and a curb which has a port angled slightly forwards.

Curb Chains

The final part of the equation with any curb bit, whether it be used with a curb, pelham or Kimblewick, is the curb chain. This acts on the curb groove, where there is said to be an acupressure point. The design you choose can have more impact than many riders realise and fitting and adjustment—as explained in the next section—is crucial.

The curb chain sold as standard with most bits is a stainless steel double link design and works perfectly well on most horses. However, some sensitive horses are much happier if you use an elastic curb chain. This is a section of strong elastic with metal rings at each end which attach it to the curb hooks.

Leather curb chains are more rigid than elastic ones and because they do not follow the contours of the chin groove, are usually not as effective. You can also buy curb chain guards, sleeves made from materials such as rubber or leather, but these add bulk and an elastic curb chain will usually be neater and more effective.

Traditionally, a curb chain should be used with a lipstrap. This is a thin, rolled leather strap which fastens to the tiny loops on curb or pelham cheeks and passes through the fly link—the single link in the centre of a curb chain which lies below the others.

It's said that the lipstrap was originally invented to prevent a curb chain falling off when a bridle is being carried, but it has a more useful purpose in helping to maintain the correct position of the chain in the curb groove.

Different types of curb chain.

Fitting and Introducing a Double

As a general guide, decide on the size of the curb bit first and choose a bradoon that is about 5mm longer, as this means that the action of one will not interfere with that of the other.

The bradoon should fit snugly into the corners of the mouth without pulling them upwards into a false 'smile'. Look inside the mouth to see if it fits comfortably, as with any other bit.

The curb should sit below and in front of the bradoon, but if you are fitting it to a gelding or stallion, be make sure it does not come into contact with the tushes. Traditional guidelines are that the curb should be 2.5cm (1in) above the tushes of a gelding and 5cm (2in) above the corner teeth of a mare.

The curb chain should be adjusted so it comes into contact when the curb is drawn back to an angle of about 45 degrees. This will usually allow an adult to fit two fingers between the curb chain and the horse's head, but double check by gently drawing back the curb rein.

Chain Reaction

A curb chain works by coming into a brief contact with the curb groove. Some people now believe that there is an acupressure point here and when light, intermittent pressure is applied here through a curb chain, it encourages the horse to relax his jaw.

If a curb chain is fitted too loosely, the curb cheeks will be drawn too far back before it comes into contact with the curb groove. If it is fastened too tightly, it will come into contact at the slightest touch of the rein and the horse will be subject to constant pressure. Depending on his temperament, he is likely to either object or switch off!

The curb chain must always lie flat against the horse. If it becomes twisted, the horse will be subject to discomfort or pain. Methods of adjusting it may alter in minor details, but one system that works is as follows:

1) Fasten the chain to the offside curb hook, with the central fly link at the bottom, and twist so it lies flat.

2) If you do not already know the fitting required for a particular horse, estimate which link will need to be hooked over.

3) Place the appropriate link over the hook so that it remains flat. As a guideline, the curb chain should come into play when rein contact moves the curb or pelham cheek to an angle of about 45 degrees.

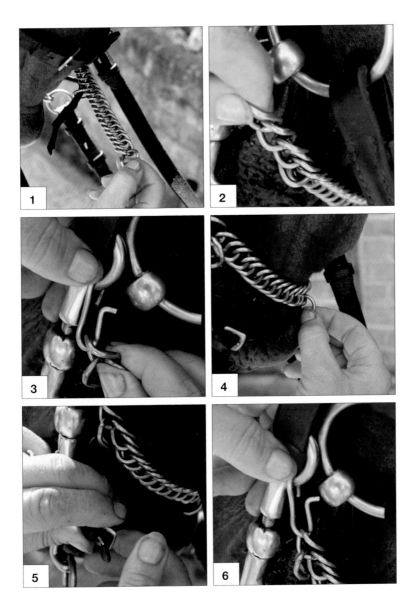

4) A lipstrap, if used, passes through the central fly link.

5) If you are using a lipstrap, buckle the short end to the small ring on the nearside bit cheek, just below the mouthpiece, and the long one to the corresponding small ring on the offside bit cheek.

6) Fasten the lipstrap just tight enough to keep the curb chain in place, without restricting its action. Check again that the curb chain is flat and at the correct tension.

Make an Introduction

It's important to introduce a double bridle carefully so that your horse gets used to its action before you use it in competition. If you haven't ridden with a double before, try and have a lesson on a horse who is schooled to work correctly in one and get an experienced trainer to help you through the process with your own horse.

When you put the bridle on, hold the bits so that the bradoon sits behind the curb. This means that each bit will lie in the correct place in the horse's mouth—though, as always, you should check again when the bridle is in place.

Give the horse time to get used to the feel of the two bits. Gently manipulating the reins from the ground will encourage him to move the bits in his mouth and relax his jaw.

Stand at the side and hold the reins under his jaw, keeping your hands in the same position as if when riding. Take a light feel on the bradoon rein and allow a small loop in the curb rein, so that only the weight of the rein plays on the bit.

Next, make a gentle play on the curb rein to encourage the horse to relax his jaw. This should be done in a give and take action; as soon as the horse responds, however slightly, release all pressure. This tells him that he has given the correct response.

Start your ridden work in walk, again riding on the bradoon rein and keeping the curb rein loose. When you're happy in walk, trot and canter, pick up the curb rein slightly but remember that the bradoon rein should be dominant.

As you and your horse gain confidence, you can ask a little more, but the rein aids should always be light and you should never feel as if you have a strong contact or are pulling the horse's head down. After a few sessions, both he and you should feel confident.

Don't ride in a double bridle all the time at home. Keep your 'normal' bit for everyday use and schooling, but ride in a double now and again to remind your horse how it feels and to maintain your dexterity.

Understanding Pelhams

The pelham also allows a curb action. Its use isn't permitted under British Dressage rules, but it is often used in the show ring and to give riders more control. If a horse or pony doesn't have room in his mouth to accommodate two bits comfortably, a pelham with two reins can be the perfect solution.

The pelham was originally designed to give the action of a double bridle, but with one mouthpiece. It is nowhere near as precise, but a lot of horses and ponies go well in it. If you use the top rein, the action echoes that of a hanging cheek snaffle, whilst the bottom rein brings a curb action into play. They should be held in the same way as the reins of a double bridle, as described earlier.

There may be occasions when a rider can't or doesn't want to use two pairs of reins. For instance, some riders prefer to have a single rein when jumping.

In these cases, it's acceptable to use a pelham with leather roundings. These are rolled leather connectors which fasten to the top and bottom rings on each side of the bit and take a single rein.

This gives a much less precise action than when two reins are used, because you are always employing a curb action. In practice, it is so limited that this doesn't cause any problems, provided that the rider keeps a light contact as a base and remembers to release and go back to it after giving a more definite signal.

Leather roundings allow a pelham to be used with a single rein.

Some horses prefer a hard rubber-covered mouthpiece, shown here on a Kimblewick (above), to a metal one (right).

Design Choices

When used correctly, a pelham isn't a severe bit, which is why so many animals go kindly in it. Again, there are lots of mouthpieces available and there are also several choices of cheekpiece.

A rubber-covered, hard mullen mouthpiece is a good one to try, as most horses seem to like it and it isn't as bulky as vulcanised rubber ones. Vulcanised rubber is treated under heat until it hardens.

There is also a variety of metal mouthpieces. In fact, if you can find a mouthpiece in a snaffle, chances are that you can also find it in a pelham.

The commonest is the mullen mouthpiece, which is slightly thinner than a rubber-covered one. A mouthpiece with a small port, often called a Cambridge mouthpiece, may be comfortable for a horse with a fleshy tongue, as it allows more room. Other examples include single- and double-jointed, lozenge, plastic, Waterford and Myler mouthpieces.

Be careful if you use a single-jointed mouthpiece. In theory, this gives the effect of riding with a hanging cheek snaffle when the top rein is used. In practice, the curb chain tends to rise out of the curb groove when the curb rein is used, which is uncomfortable for the horse.

As with the curb of a double bridle, the length of a pelham cheek affects the amount of leverage that can be applied—so the longer the cheek, the greater the potential severity of the bit. Again, the standard ratio used by manufacturers is that the length of the cheeks equals the length of the mouthpiece.

Pelham with Myler mouthpiece.

Be careful when fitting pelhams to horses and ponies with broad muzzles, such as cobs and heavier native breeds. You may find that with some bits, the rings which take the bridle cheekpieces dig into the side of the horse's face. Some manufacturers angle the rings away from the face to avoid this, so you may need to compare different bits.

If your horse tries to grab the bottom rings of a pelham, look for one with Scamperdale cheeks. These are angled back from the mouthpiece to prevent this. Grabbing at the rings is not just annoying, but potentially dangerous, as it's possible for one of the bottom, small rings to become lodged over the horse's teeth.

Pelham with Scamperdale angled-back cheeks.

Rugby pelham.

Pelham Puzzlers

Professional riders, particularly show producers, often have a huge variety of pelhams. Most of us will never use most of these designs, but it's interesting to understand how they are designed to work.

The SM pelham and the Swales three-in-one are two in particular that you may see in real life or in magazine and website pictures. The first looks more fearsome than it is and the second is not recommended for general use.

The SM pelham takes the initials of its inventor, Sam Marsh. It has a broad, flat mouthpiece with a central port, which gives a good bearing area without bulk. The cheeks move independently, though the movement is limited.

This makes it a good option for animals which tend to lean on the bit and bear down on the reins in certain circumstances, such as when galloping in company. As such, you may see it used on horses such as show cobs.

The Swales three-in-one is a very different prospect. This has rings set inside the curb cheeks, to which the bridle cheekpieces and the top rein attach. The bottom rein goes to the curb rings. This bit applies minimum poll pressure, but the inside rings have a squeezing action. When the curb rein is applied, the bit revolves in the mouth.

The Rugby pelham, which has loose rings set outside the mouthpiece, is very different and often suits a horse

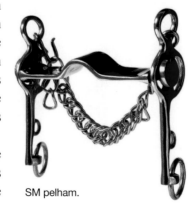

SM pelham.

who likes a little more play in the mouthpiece. It usually has a ported mouthpiece, which allows room for the tongue.

Showing riders often use a Rugby pelham with a bridle sliphead. This gives a similar appearance to a double bridle and some believe it makes the horse's head look more 'finished.'

However, using a sliphead means that the bit does not act as it is designed to. The movement of the loose rings is restricted and you bring in a degree of poll pressure. Having said that, some horses go very well when it is used this way, so it's a case of trying and seeing.

The Kimblewick

As the hanging cheek snaffle has come into popularity, so the Kimblewick has enjoyed a revival. This bit is, perhaps, a cross between a snaffle and a pelham, as the rings offer so limited a leverage that using this bit is equivalent to riding on the top rein of a pelham—so by definition, it acts on the poll.

The action of a Uttoxeter Kimblewick, which has slots in the rings, is slightly different. If the reins are attached to the top slot, the action is similar to other Kimblewicks. If they are fastened to the bottom one, the action of the bit is always directly on the bars of the mouth, which some horses find uncomfortable.

Kimblewicks are also available with a wide choice of mouthpieces. Most have a port mouthpiece.

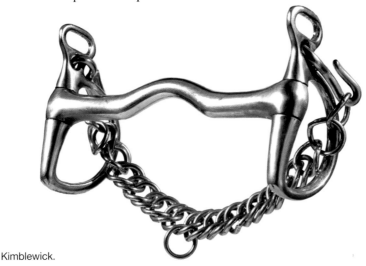

Kimblewick.

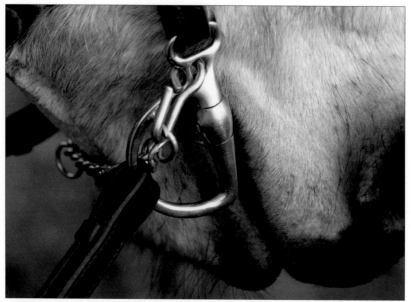

Threading the curb chain through the bit rings helps keep it in the correct place.

Curb Chains

Although a Kimblewick applies limited curb action, you also have the option of using an elastic or other design of curb chain.

When using a curb chain with a pelham or Kimblewick, there are two possible fittings. One is to pass the curb chain behind the top ring and the other is to slot it through the offside ring and back out through the nearside one. The second method helps to keep the curb chain lying in the correct place, in the curb groove.

When gauging the fit of a curb chain with a pelham, the most accurate way is to adjust it so it comes into contact when the bit cheeks are drawn back to an angle of 45 degrees. With a Kimblewick, it's easier to adjust it so that you can fit two fingers between the chain and the horse's face.

Driving Bits

Although this book concentrates on bits relating to ridden animals, there may be some readers who are interested in taking up driving. In this discipline, you'll find far fewer bits in use.

Possible reasons for this are that drivers—traditionally known as whips—make a fuller use of voice signals than most riders. Also, whilst driving horses have to be manoeuvrable, especially when negotiating cones and obstacle courses in competition, they are not asked to perform movements beyond those required in a novice dressage test, with the exception of rein-back.

The traditional driving bit, which is still in common use, is the Liverpool bit. This usually has a straight bar mouthpiece, though others are available. A straight bar mouthpiece is not popular for riding, because it puts pressure directly on the bars and does not allow room for the tongue. However, remember that a whip sits above the horse and as such, the angle of the reins is different from when a horse is ridden and bar pressure is therefore lessened.

The Liverpool bit has a choice of rein positions that allow less or greater potential leverage and is used with a curb chain. Its versatility meant that grooms could change over teams of horses quickly, without having to change bits, when time was of the essence. It also gives a uniformity of appearance to turnouts drawn by two or more horses.

Liverpool driving bit.

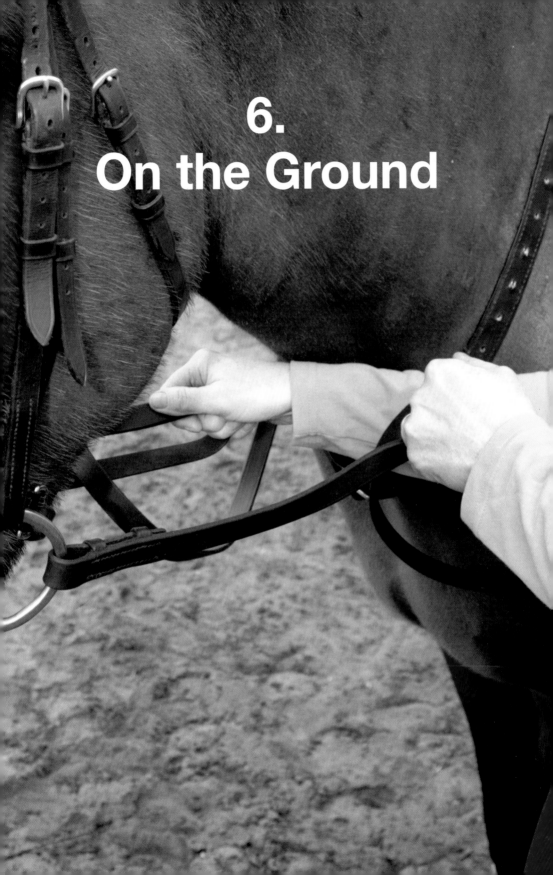

6.
On the Ground

You need to think about choosing and using bits when you are working with a horse or pony on the ground, as well as under saddle. Perhaps you are involved with showing a youngster in hand as part of his education, or even with backing him. Lungeing and long reining also bring in bitting issues to consider.

Starting Out

Introducing a young horse to the bit should be done carefully and considerately. After all, you're asking him to accept what must be a strange experience; until now, everything that has gone into his mouth has been edible!

Horses have to be taught both to accept a bit and to respond to it. In both cases, time and patience will reap long-term dividends and impatience will set up problems. Unfortunately, time constraints are often put on the backing/starting procedure—usually because an owner is paying for someone else to do it and has to set a limit on the cost—but whilst you have to be realistic, remember that investing in the foundation of a youngster's education will reap dividends later on.

'Making a horse's mouth', as trainers often term this introductory process, isn't rocket science. It means that you teach a horse to accept a bit in his mouth and to respond to gentle signals so that he learns to move between paces, halt and change direction before a rider gets on board.

This way, he does not have to cope with adjusting to a rider's balance at the same time. Learning a new skill is always easiest when it is broken down into small steps, whether you are a horse or a human!

Don't underestimate the importance of building this communication via a bit. It is, of course, just part of the picture. Voice commands and body language play an important role in groundwork and voice commands help you continue that clear communication both when you start riding a young horse and later on.

As with all skills, you need to understand what you are trying to achieve when educating a horse to the bit. When you advance to lungeing with side reins and, perhaps, long reining, you also need to be proficient and confident before trying to train a horse. The best way to learn is to find a good instructor who can teach you what to do with the help of an experienced horse.

Showing in-hand, using a mild bit and a tactful hand.

Bit by Bit

Unfortunately, we back and train young horses at a time when their mouths are in a permanent stage of change, as they don't have a full set of adult teeth until they are five years old. Before you think about introducing a bit, get your horse's mouth checked by your vet or EDT to make sure that there are no problems which mean it would be sensible to wait a little longer.

Opinions differ as to the age at which a bit should be introduced. If you intend to show a yearling colt in hand, many societies and shows stipulate that all colts and stallions should be bitted; otherwise, many people wait until a horse is two years old or, depending on their management methods, until the youngster is shown in hand or even when the backing process starts. It isn't so much the age that matters as the way the process is carried out and the way the horse is handled.

Starter Bit

At one time, a special bit with keys attached to the centre of the mouthpiece, called a breaking or mouthing bit, was used to start a horse's education (*see* page 77). The idea was that the keys would encourage him to play with the bit, salivate and accept it.

Hollow mouth snaffle.

Some trainers still use this, particularly if a horse seems to have a dry mouth. However, it can be counterproductive, as it may encourage a horse to fiddle with the bit—a habit that may continue into his ridden work. As there are now many materials that are said to encourage salivation, the traditional mouthing bit often isn't needed.

Unless you have a particular reason for using a mouthing bit, the only bit suitable for use when starting a horse's education is a simple snaffle. There are no hard and fast rules about which design is best, though it should be as thick as is suitable for your horse's mouth conformation, to allow a greater bearing area. It also seems logical to use one that stays central in the horse's mouth and minimises the risk of pinching or of the mouthpiece pulling through to one side, such as an eggbutt, full cheek or D-ring snaffle.

If you use a metal bit, which some trainers prefer to do, then it's obvious that the thicker a solid mouthpiece is, the heavier the weight of the bit. A hollow mouth snaffle is much lighter and may be accepted more readily.

A lightweight plastic or nylon unjointed mouthpiece suits many horses as a starter bit. Youngsters vary in their response to a bit: some accept it as if they have been wearing it for months whilst others find it very frustrating and are convinced that if they try long enough, they'll manage to spit it out. The advantage of an unjointed plastic mouthpiece is that it makes it less likely that a horse will put his tongue over the bit.

Lightweight plastic mouthpiece

Breaking bit with keys.

Making the Introduction

It's important to introduce a bridle and bit sympathetically and without fuss. Do it in the horse's stable, having taken out any mangers or buckets so there is nothing to get caught on a bridle, but if for some reason he hasn't been stabled before, get him accustomed to this first.

For the sake of safety, always wear a hard hat and suitable footwear when handling your young horse, and wear gloves when leading, lungeing or long reining, no matter how quiet and amenable he is. This way, you minimise the risk of injury if he steps on your toe or throws up his head when you're standing next to him.

Begin by removing the noseband and reins from your bridle and get your horse used to having the headpiece passed over his ears. The browband must be long enough to avoid any risk of the base of his ears being pinched, which often means mixing and matching bridle parts. For instance, a small native pony with a broad forehead may need a cob-size or even a full-size browband with a pony-size headpiece and cheekpieces.

The next step is to attach the bit and try and gauge the appropriate height by holding the bridle against the side of the horse's head. You're now ready to introduce the bit; again, there isn't a hard and fast technique, but the method described here works well.

Stand on the nearside of his head and hold the cheekpieces together in your right hand. Position the bit just below your horse's nose so that he can investigate it. Nine times out of ten, a horse will explore the bit with his mouth, but if he is one of the rare few who ignores it, try coating the mouthpiece with honey or molasses, as the smell will prompt his interest. You can support the bit with your left hand if necessary, but

77

don't push it against the horse's mouth. You're inviting him to take it, not telling him that he must do so—a little patience will pay off.

As he takes the bit, ease it gently into his mouth and slide the headpiece over his ears, keeping your movements smooth and quiet. You can then adjust the height of the bit, if necessary, and fasten the throatlatch.

In most cases, it's as simple as that. If a horse ignores the bit and doesn't open his mouth, even when the mouthpiece is coated in something sweet, slip your finger into the side of his mouth and tickle his tongue. This often works better than pressing down on the bars of his mouth.

For his first experience, let him get used to the unaccustomed feel of the bit for a few minutes. Stay with him, as even when you've taken out obvious hazards, he may try and rub his face and get the bridle or bit rings caught. Over the next few days, you can then increase the time he wears it until he happily accepts it for around 15 minutes.

Starting to Signal

You can now teach a horse to accept and respond to the bit, first through simple leading and later through lungeing and long reining. Again, different trainers have different methods, but the one suggested here is effective. All early lessons should be carried out in a safe, fenced environment, preferably an arena or round pen.

Before you use any signals through the bit, teach your horse to respond to simple walk and halt commands through voice commands and body language when he is wearing a headcollar. If you aren't sure how to do this, ask a good instructor who is used to working with horses at the start of their education to help you.

From there, it's a case of combining gentle but clear pressure and release signals via the bit with the commands he already knows. To make things even clearer, and to avoid putting too much pressure on his mouth, attach your lead rein to a coupling which fastens to the bit rings and to the noseband.

These are often used for showing youngsters in hand and combine the new signals with pressure on the nose, a control point he already understands from being led in a headcollar. It's up to you whether you use a lead rein or rope—preferably an extra long one to give you more control—or a lunge line.

A coupling which attaches to the noseband and the bit rings helps avoid unwanted pressure on the mouth.

Introducing Side Reins

Using side reins whilst lungeing teaches a horse to accept a light contact on the bit. First, he must be taught to lunge wearing a lunge cavesson, minus side reins, with the lunge rein attached to the cavesson.

Always start every lunge session without side reins, even when working an experienced horse. This gives him time to move his head and neck freely as he starts to move and his muscles warm up.

There are three basic designs of side rein: plain leather or webbing and leather or webbing with an either an elastic insert or an inset rubber ring. Avoid using side reins which are made from very lightweight, flimsy webbing, as these can flap around and cause unwanted movement of the bit.

Side reins attached to a cavesson.

There are no hard and fast rules about whether you should use plain side reins or ones with inserts, though different trainers have different views. However, as we all try and ride with an elastic contact rather than with rigid hands, it seems logical that side reins with strong elastic inserts—which offer a small amount of give—mimic that. Side reins with rubber rings tend to bounce up and down, which again causes unwanted movement of the bit.

Some trainers believe that plain side reins are better than ones with elastic inserts for horses which try and lean on the bit when lunged. It's often a case of assessing your horse and, if you think a different design might help, trying it to see which seems more productive.

You may want to start by attaching side reins to the side rings of the lunge cavesson, so that the horse gets used to the idea of working within a frame through a contact on the nose, rather than on the bit.

Adjusting Side Reins

Most horses accept side reins without any resistance as long as they are adjusted correctly. When you are using them for the first time, start by using an outside rein only—so if you are lungeing on the left rein, where the horse describes an anti-clockwise circle, you will start with a single side rein attached on the right hand side. When he is confident, add a second side rein.

You can adjust side reins at different heights, especially if you are using a lunge roller with several side rings rather than using a saddle and attaching them to the girth. In general, and definitely with a young horse, they should be attached to a lower fitting; as a rule of thumb, fasten them so they are level with the point of the shoulder.

To gauge the correct length, stand the horse so that his nose is just in front of the vertical. When you clip the side reins to the cavesson rings or bit rings, there should be a light contact as he stands in that position. If in doubt, it's better to have them a little loose rather than too tight.

As the horse progresses in his training, you can shorten the side reins so that there is a light contact when he stands with his nose on the vertical. There should never be more than a light contact on the bit and they should never be used to try and force an outline by pulling in his head.

Side reins should be of equal length. If you are having trouble establishing the correct bend on one rein, ask your instructor to help you gain more influence through your stance and signals with the lunge whip.

Long Reining and Lungeing with Two Reins

As your young horse's training progresses, you may want to long rein him to introduce the idea of steering before a rider gets on. This is a skill that must be learned from an experienced and accomplished trainer, to avoid putting unwanted pressure on the horse's mouth.

Long reining can be carried out on straight lines or on a circle, though you will see different terms used to describe these activities. For instance, some trainers refer to long reining on a circle as double lungeing and to long reining on a straight line as driving.

In both cases, you can use two good quality lunge reins, though some trainers say that leather driving reins or reins made from marine ply rope allow more sensitive handling. Again, you can introduce the idea by fastening the reins to the side rings of a lunge cavesson rather than to the bit rings. Always introduce the long reins one at a time in safe surroundings, moving them gently along the horse's body until he accepts them quietly—and always stand out of kicking distance, as the quietest

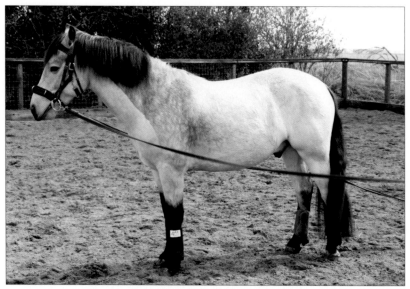

Long reining is a useful way of working a horse from the ground.

horse may be startled by the initial feel of the rein against his body.

Many trainers prefer to use a rubber or 'plastic' bit when long reining a young horse, surmising that it is kinder to the horse's mouth, though an established animal can wear a simple snaffle of any suitable design. Don't use a bit which employs any degree of leverage.

As your hands are lower than when you are riding, the bit has a more direct action on the bars and, because you are so far away, there is the potential for more pressure to be exerted. This makes it important to keep a soft contact, so keep your elbows bent, as when riding. If you straighten your arms, the muscles become tense.

Lungeing with two reins gives you the opportunity to introduce the idea of using an inside and an outside rein—again, before a young horse has the added complication of a rider's weight. It isn't within the scope of this book to go into details of techniques, but there is a lot of value in working a horse on the ground from the bit.

Everyone has to start some time, so try and achieve the necessary dexterity and correct positioning of your body with the help of a good trainer and an experienced horse. There is also a growing interest in classical in-hand work and some trainers are experts in teaching lateral work in hand. Again, this should be started in a snaffle, though an expert trainer may work an advanced horse in hand in a double bridle.

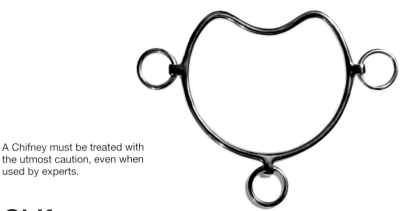

A Chifney must be treated with the utmost caution, even when used by experts.

Chifney

In some situations, you may be advised to use a Chifney when leading a horse. Whilst it may be true that every bit has a use if it is in expert hands, this is one that should not be in general use and even in the hands of an expert, should be treated with the utmost caution.

It was designed in the 18th century by Samuel Chifney, a jockey, and its original purpose was as an anti-rearing bit, primarily for colts and stallions. Some people recommend its use for horses who are difficult to load, though this view is now less prevalent.

This ring-shaped bit has a thin mouthpiece and encircles the lower jaw. It attaches to a headpiece and should be used with a long lead rope or lunge rein fastened to the back ring, behind the jaw.

The principle behind it is that when a horse walks calmly, there must be no pressure on the rope or rein. However, if he attempts to rear or take off, the mouthpiece exerts a strong downward pressure. As soon as he stops or stands without resistance, the pressure must be removed.

Safety is obviously paramount, which is why most handlers and trainers would never say never about the Chifney! But whilst you must be in control, forceful handling—which is very different from a firm approach—is, as a general principle, unacceptable. It is also unproductive, as causing discomfort or even pain will increase unwanted behaviour rather than prevent it.

If you know a horse is difficult to lead or load, the most productive route is usually to train him to respond to the principles of pressure and release in safe surroundings, if necessary with a knowledgeable trainer. Don't take unnecessary risks and remember to wear a safety hat, appropriate footwear, gloves and, if necessary, a body protector.

7. Other Considerations

Cavesson noseband.

Cavesson with padded double-back fastening to minimise pressure.

By now, you will have reached the stage where you know how to decide which bits might be suitable for a particular horse or pony. In many cases, you will usually end up with a shortlist.

You can then find one or more that, when looked at as part of the overall picture, may help your horse's way of going. But before you start buying or borrowing, there is one other piece of the puzzle to slot into place: the effect of other equipment on a bit's action. This includes nosebands; combination bits with built-in nosebands; variations on bridle design and martingales.

On the Nose

Most nosebands, with the exception of the cavesson noseband, are designed to prevent the horse opening his mouth too wide. As such, they fit above and below the bit. Not all designs are permitted in all disciplines, so check rule books.

There is an important distinction between the purpose stated above and fastening the horse's mouth shut. For a horse to accept the bit and work on the bit, he must be relaxed in his jaw. If his jaws are restricted by a too tight noseband, this is impossible.

Some horses dislike any noseband which fastens below the bit and will work much better if ridden in a plain cavesson. If your horse is resisting your rein aids and you've ruled out possible causes—notably mouth discomfort and riding technique—try a simple cavesson in safe, enclosed surroundings. You may be pleasantly surprised.

If your horse accepts the bit and works correctly and happily, there is no compelling reason to use a noseband other than for aesthetic reasons. Most English-style riders feel that without a noseband, a horse's head looks unfinished and that a cavesson noseband gives a smarter appearance. A noseband is compulsory for all Pony Club activities.

However, Western-style riders don't use nosebands. This is mainly due to tradition, but also because this style of riding should rely on minimum mouth pressure—particularly when a curb bit is used, as is the case with educated horses—and as such, horses should be less likely to resist the bit.

A young horse who is teething may show mouth resistances through discomfort. First, check that it will not cause problems to continue working him and if there is any doubt, wait until the teeth causing the problem have erupted. If you are using a metal bit, a lightweight, plastic mouthpiece may be more comfortable for the horse.

It may be that a noseband is causing discomfort by pressing on sensitive areas and that the horse will be comfortable if you remove it or, if necessary, use a high-ring Grakle (*see* page 90.) You may also be able to use a bitless bridle as a temporary measure, as explained in Chapter 8.

Flash noseband.

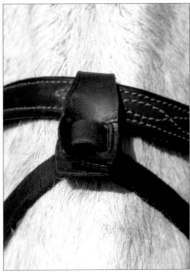

Flash converter.

Drop noseband (from different angles).

Nosebands in Action

A **cavesson** noseband may be used mainly for the sake of appearance, but you still need to be careful about adjustment and fitting. Make sure it sits below the facial bones, so there is no danger of rubbing, and that you can comfortably fit two fingers between it and the horse's face.

If your horse has a short muzzle and you want to use a full cheek snaffle, you may find that the top of the cheekpieces could become trapped under the noseband. In this case, either use keepers to hold the cheeks in the correct place or try a D-ring bit instead.

A **cinch** noseband, sometimes called a **double-back**, is designed so it can be pulled tighter than an ordinary cavesson one. As discomfort causes problems, the design is illogical.

Don't confuse this noseband with padded nosebands designed to relieve pressure which incorporate double-back fastenings. Here, the double-back design adds to the buffering layers between the metal buckle and the horse's face. A loosely fastened ordinary cinch or double-back noseband should also be comfortable for the horse.

A **Flash** noseband is a cavesson with a strap at the centre front which fastens below the bit. It has a vague action, as there is no definite control point, though this is probably why it is effective on some horses! It also helps to keep the bit central in the horse's mouth and because of this, some trainers like to use it as standard, especially with horses who are ridden in loose ring snaffles.

On a purpose-made Flash, the drop strap passes through a loop or is stitched to the cavesson section. There is also the option of a Flash converter—a piece of leather with slots which folds over a cavesson noseband—but this is often unsatisfactory, as the bottom strap may rest too low. If you use a Flash noseband, choose one with a substantial cavesson section, as this helps to prevent it slipping down the horse's face.

The top part of a Flash may be fitted slightly tighter than an ordinary cavesson to help give stability, but it should not restrict the horse when he is not resisting and you should be able to fit two fingers between the drop strap and the face.

The **drop** noseband comes into and out of fashion. If its proportions complement those of the horse's head and it is adjusted correctly, it can be more useful than many riders realise. It has a more definite action than the Flash noseband. The back strap sits in the curb groove, so when a horse attempts to open his mouth too far, he meets resistance. At the same time, the front strap applies pressure on the nose, which encourages the horse to bring in his head.

The top strap should not be so long that it interferes with the bit rings, but nor should it be so short that the cheek straps are pulled too far forwards. The best designs are adjustable at the back and front, but are hard to find and you may need to have such a noseband made to order.

The most important consideration when fitting a drop noseband is to ensure that it does not restrict the horse's breathing. The front strap must sit on the nasal bone, not in the soft nostril area below. Some designs include small leather inserts linking the front strap with the cheek straps, which prevent the front strap dropping down, but unfortunately few manufacturers now include this.

When a drop noseband is fastened, you should be able to fit two fingers between it and the horse's face. If a horse manages to get his tongue over the bit when wearing a drop noseband, it is important to unfasten the noseband and rectify this immediately, as he may react badly. If a horse habitually puts his tongue over the bit, run through all the checks in Chapter 2 and, if necessary, ask advice. A drop noseband makes it more difficult for the horse to put his tongue back in the correct position once he has moved it over the bit, so if this happens regularly, use another design.

The **Grakle** noseband, also called a **crossover** or **figure-of-eight**, is popular with those riding and training three- to five-year-olds, as it minimises the risk of pressure on sensitive areas when a horse is

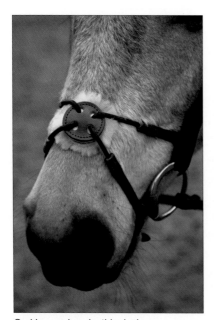

Grakle noseband – this design incorporates elastic to minimise pressure.

High-ring Grakle, sometimes called an American or Mexican Grakle.

cutting teeth. There are two versions: the original Grakle and the high-ring version, sometimes called a Mexican or American Grakle. The top straps of the latter originate higher up the face, which means there is no pressure on the cheek teeth.

The control point of a Grakle noseband is higher up the face, where the noseband crosses. The junction must be padded—most designs use sheepskin—or pressure is imposed on a very small area. This noseband can be effective on horses who cross their jaws as an evasion, but be careful that it is not fastened too tightly, or it may add to the problem rather than help resolve it.

Latest Thoughts

It is not intended to endorse individual products, but both the **Micklem Multibridle** and the **Myler combination bit** should be recognised and their actions appreciated.

The Micklem Multibridle can be used with or without a bit and the version with a ring on the centre of the noseband can also be used as a lunge cavesson. When used with a bit, it avoids pressure on areas which are sensitive when a young horse is teething. The noseband fastens below

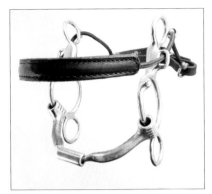

Myler combination bit.

Micklem Multibridle, fitted here for lungeing.

the bit but, because it is contoured, the bridle is easier to fit than one with a conventional drop noseband.

The Myler combination bit includes a hide or leather noseband and back strap and works on both the nose, mouth and jaw areas. Although it may be used successfully on strong horses, many riders feel that it is not severe and that the different control points and adjustment options allow control without undue pressure. Some trainers like to use this as a early bit for young horses, because its action includes nose pressure—something a young horse is accustomed to from being led in a headcollar.

Direct Action

Some nosebands have a potentially severe action. They are not recommended for general use and may not be permitted under Pony Club rules, so check before using them. Even if you never use them, you may see them, particularly on horses going cross country.

The **lever** noseband, also called the **crescent** or **combination** noseband, comprises a front section with a metal core, two curved metal arms which fit in front of the bit and two back straps. The top back strap fastens at the back of the jaw above the bit and the bottom strap is secured below the bit.

When a firm contact is taken on the reins, strong pressure is exerted on the nose and jaw. Don't confuse this noseband with the Myler combination bit.

The **Kineton** or **Puckle** noseband has a central strap with a u-shaped metal loop at each end and was designed for use on a horse who pulls. When a contact is taken on the reins, pressure is applied on the nose and the metal loops squeeze inwards against the sides of the mouth.

Its inventor recommended that it be used with a mullen mouth snaffle—not a bit with a jointed mouthpiece, or with any form of curb bit. The reason is that with a mullen mouth snaffle, pressure is applied to the nose before the bit comes into full play.

The Kineton or Puckle noseband has a central strap with a U-shaped metal loop at each end.

The nose pressure gives the horse a warning to slow down, so if he obeys, the rein contact must be lightened immediately, but not 'thrown away.' If he doesn't respond, pressure is also applied through the control points of the mouth.

Martingales

Both the **running** and **bib** martingales have an effect on the bit, as they are linked to the reins. The **standing** martingale does not, as it is attached to a cavesson noseband or to the cavesson part of a Flash.

The **Irish** martingale, a short strap with a ring at each end through which the reins pass, is used mainly in racing and the idea is that if a rider falls, the reins will not go over the horse's head and cause him to trip or fall. It has very little effect on the reins other than limiting the extent to which a rider can open a rein to the side.

Many riders use a martingale—particularly a running martingale—as standard, especially when hacking or jumping. There is nothing wrong with this and a correctly fitted running martingale can actually increase a horse's comfort when he is being ridden by a novice or unbalanced rider, as it acts as a buffer between unwanted movements of the reins and the horse's mouth.

It also means you have a neckstrap available if needed. If you need to

Standing martingale.

Running martingale.

Bib martingale.

use a breastplate with your saddle, you can buy ones which also have martingale attachments.

However, it's important to ride without a martingale sometimes, especially when schooling on the flat in safe surroundings. A martingale can give a false picture of a horse's way of going and, of course, you are not allowed to use one in a dressage test. By all means use one when jumping—in fact, some trainers feel it is safest to do so—but do at least some of your work on the flat without one, as long as you are safe and in control.

How They Work

A martingale is designed to come into effect when a horse raises his head above the angle of control, not to hold his head down.

The running martingale attaches to the girth at one end, then splits into two straps, each with a ring at the end through which the reins pass. A neckstrap helps keep it in place and can be useful in its own right; if your horse is on the forehand or rushing, slip one hand under the neckstrap and 'take and give' to encourage him to re-balance himself.

A rubber stop must be used to prevent a martingale dropping between the horse's legs.

This does not put pressure on the mouth and applies a rudimentary half halt. It is particularly useful with young and sensitive horses.

A bib martingale is similar in design to a running martingale, but the straps which connect to the reins are joined by a triangular piece of leather or leather and elastic. It has a more definite action but limits the extent to which you can open the reins, though designs incorporating elastic offer a little more leeway. It is the only design safe to use on a horse who tries to grab hold of a running martingale.

All martingales must be used with rubber stops for safety. One links the neckstrap with the strap running to the girth, to prevent the girth strap dropping too low between the horse's front legs. The others fit on the reins to prevent the rings slipping too far down and possibly catching on the billets, or on the bottom ring of a pelham or a curb bit. Some riders like to use two stops on each rein, to limit the movement of the rings still farther.

If by any chance you need to use a running or bib martingale with a double bridle, or a pelham with two reins, then traditionally it should be attached to the curb (bottom) rein, not to the snaffle (top) one, so as to complement the bit's action. However, some riders prefer to use it on the snaffle rein.

When a martingale is correctly fitted, you should be able to fit a hand's width between the neckstrap and your horse's neck. The strap which runs to the girth should be fed through the rubber stop to the point where it doesn't pull against the horse at the chest and between his front legs, which would make him uncomfortable and restrict his movement, but does not hang too far down.

It's important to make sure that the martingale comes into play when needed, but does not exert permanent downward pressure. One guideline that is often recommended is to attach the martingale to the girth, then take both rings to one side. When the straps are stretched taut, the rings should reach almost to the withers.

If a horse has a particularly sloping or particularly straight shoulder, or has particularly high or flat withers, you may get a better first fit by taking the rings along the underside of the horse's neck so the rings reach the gullet. Whatever method you use, always check the fit again when the rider is mounted. When the horse's head is at a correct working height and the rider holds the reins so that there is a straight line from the elbow to the horse's mouth, there should not be a kink in the reins.

Correctly fitted martingale neckstrap.

8.
Bitless Bridles

It may seem contradictory to have information about bitless bridles in a book that focuses on choosing and using bits, but it's a subject every rider needs to know about.

There may be times when you need to keep working a horse but can't use a bit, perhaps because he is uncomfortable when cutting teeth, or if he has a mouth ulcer or small injury. If in doubt as to whether or not you should work the horse, ask your vet.

There are also riders who choose to ride bitless for some or all of the time. For instance, some trainers prefer to use a bitless bridle during a horse's early education, so the horse can adjust to a rider's weight without the risk of inadvertent mouth pressure.

Riding with a bitless bridle in safe surroundings, on a horse who is known to go kindly and under the supervision of a teacher who understands the techniques involved, can be a useful short-term exercise. However experienced you are, it reminds you of the importance of using your weight aids and highlights how easy it is to put too much reliance on the reins.

A minority of riders chooses to ride bitless all the time. These riders believe that this a kinder method, though there is no reason why a horse who is correctly ridden with a bit that has been chosen according to the principles explained in this book should be caused discomfort. A bitless bridle that is incorrectly-fitted or used may itself cause discomfort or pain.

Scawbrig.

Pressure points of a Blair's pattern or English hackamore.

Designs in Action

There are many designs of bitless bridle, but a core of tried and tested designs remains in common use. One of the simplest is the Scawbrig. This comprises a strap with rings at each end which fits across the nose and a back strap which passes through the rings, behind the jaw and fastens to the reins. This applies pressure on the nose, the sides of the face and the jaw.

The Blair's pattern bridle, more often known as the English hackamore, has a leather strap across the front of the nose attached to metal arms and a curb strap or curb chain behind the jaw. The reins and bridle cheekpieces attach to the metal arms and transfer pressure to the nose, jaw and poll.

The German hackamore, which is similar in design to the English one but with much longer metal arms, is capable of exerting considerable leverage. In good hands, it can be used with success in situations which need fine control, such as showjumping.

Crossover bitless bridles, which are a newer design, spread pressure over a wider area than other bitless bridles. The Micklem Multibridle, which is permitted under Pony Club rules when used with a snaffle, converts to two types of bitless bridle; one adaptation is similar to the Scawbrig and the other is a crossover design.

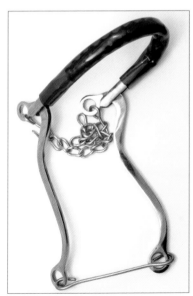
German hackamore.

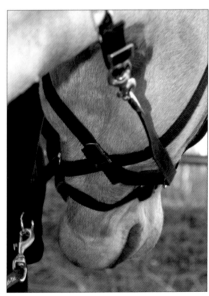
Crossover bitless bridle.

Fit to Go

All bitless bridles must be adjusted so that, as with a drop noseband, the front part does not restrict the horse's breathing. A rider who uses one on a particular horse all the time may need to raise or lower it a hole occasionally to prevent rubs. You can also use sheepskin sleeves on the noseband and/or the curb chain or curb strap if necessary.

If you use an English or German hackamore, check that the noseband and back strap are tensioned correctly. As a starting point, adjust them so that they act on the nose and jaw when the arms are at an angle of 45 degrees. Don't fasten them too loosely in the mistaken belief that this is a milder setting. If the jaw strap or chain is too loose, the pressure on the nose and jaw will be too abrupt.

Riding Bitless

It's true that a correctly-schooled horse in the hands of a good rider who is experienced at riding bitless should be able to do anything without a bit that he can do with one. This includes adopting the posture and way of going that would otherwise be described as on the bit, as he can still work from behind, lift his abdominal muscles and go in a light, balanced way.

However, you will need help to achieve a harmonious way of going and be prepared to practise. Always start in a safe, enclosed area and get help from an instructor who can help you with fitting the bridle and with riding technique.

- Riding bitless does not have to mean riding with loose, hanging reins. The following pointers may help:
- Stay soft through your arms, elbows, wrists and shoulders, with a light feel on the reins—just as you would as if you were riding with a bit.
- If your horse stays soft through his neck, you don't need to ask for any more. If he becomes or is habitually a little stiff through the neck, open your hands and ask him to soften by squeezing and releasing the reins.
- Think ahead and be aware of your weight aids. You may find that you need to ask your horse to turn earlier than if you were riding with a bit, especially when jumping.
- When you turn, bring the outside hand to the neck and open your inside hand.

9. Last Word

Hopefully, this book will help you realise that choosing and using a bit doesn't have to be overwhelmingly complicated. It will take a lot of thought, but you should now be able to make sure that your horse is comfortable, that you are in control and can communicate with him.

Whether you're choosing a bit for a young horse or trying to solve a schooling problem, here's a final checklist. If in doubt, get expert advice. By all means listen to different opinions, but only take advice from those whose knowledge and experience you can be sure of.

1) Make sure your horse's mouth and teeth are in good condition through regular checks from a good equine vet or EDT. If you suspect there might be a problem, schedule an immediate check—don't wait for a routine visit.

2) Assess your horse's mouth conformation.

3) Learn how different bits work and how the design of a mouthpiece or cheekpiece can affect a bit's action.

4) Make sure a bit is the correct size and is adjusted at the correct height.

5) If you are having a schooling problem, start with point 1) and also check that your horse isn't resisting the bit because of problems elsewhere in his body. This will often mean involving your vet and/or other professionals such as a farrier or saddle fitter.

6) Check that your riding isn't causing or compounding a problem. None of us is perfect and it often takes a good instructor to point out that our position or the way we give an aid is causing imbalance or resistance.

7) Be aware of the way nosebands and martingales can affect a bit's action

8) If necessary, check that any bits and bridles you use are permitted under Pony Club and other relevant rules.

9) If you are happy with the way your horse goes in a particular bit, don't change it for the sake of change. Equally, be prepared to use different bits for different disciplines or activities.

10) Listen to your horse. He can't read books, but his reactions and behaviour will tell you how he feels!

Index